STUDIES IN HISTORY, ECONOMICS AND PUBLIC LAW

Edited by the

**FACULTY OF POLITICAL SCIENCE
OF COLUMBIA UNIVERSITY**

NUMBER 383

JOHANN GOTTLIEB FICHTE

A STUDY OF HIS POLITICAL WRITINGS WITH SPECIAL
REFERENCE TO HIS NATIONALISM

BY

H. C. ENGELBRECHT

JOHANN GOTTLIEB FICHTE

A Study of his political writings with special reference to his Nationalism

BY

H. C. ENGELBRECHT

AMS PRESS
NEW YORK

Reprinted with the permission of Columbia University Press
From the edition of 1933, New York
First AMS EDITION published 1968
Manufactured in the United States of America

Library of Congress Catalogue Card Number: 68-54262

AMS PRESS, INC.
New York, N.Y. 10003

TABLE OF CONTENTS

ACKNOWLEDGMENT

This study owes much to the helpful suggestions and ready advice of Professor Carlton J. H. Hayes. I am glad to make this grateful acknowledgment.

H. C. ENGELBRECHT.

INTRODUCTION

STATING THE PROBLEM

" FICHTE as political philosopher! A flood of writings on this subject has appeared and been spread. . . It is amusing to see how Fichte is pronounced now a democrat, and then a socialist. One group extols him as a cosmopolite, another as the most ardent patriot. On the one hand he is proclaimed a pacifist, praising with Kant eternal peace; on the other he is a nationalist, pronouncing with Machiavelli that war is an ethical duty. One group invokes him as spokesman for the League of Nations, the other sees in him a prophet of the German national state of the future. . . What are the facts? " [1] In this manner Johnsen summarized the problem of the Fichte student.

In Germany the situation is particularly confused, because Fichte today is being pressed into service for purposes of political propaganda. Almost every party believes it has a claim on him and cites from his works whatever suits its needs. This practice, naturally, is not conducive to objective evaluation of Fichte's political thought.[2]

The whole situation is vividly illuminated by a reference to the World War. Within a hair's breadth Fichte missed joining that satanic trinity, Nietzsche, Treitschke, and Bernhardi, as an outstanding cause of the war. He did not, in fact, escape the charge, as a few examples will demonstrate.

[1] Helmuth Johnsen, *Das Staatsideal J. G. Fichtes* (Neustadt bei Coburg, 1929), p. 7.

[2] On this post-war German situation, see Chapter VIII.

Santayana's *Egotism in German Philosophy,* though appearing in war time (1916), and thus partially at least a product of the war, is none the less " the fruit of long gestation." [3]   Santayana declares that he has always felt something " sinister at work, something at once hollow and aggressive " under the " obscure and fluctuating tenets " of German metaphysics.   He devotes an entire chapter to Fichte, which dwells on the self-glorification of the Germans and abounds in references to the World War.[4]   Fichte emerges as the champion of the tyrannical power of the state over the individual, the prophet of German racial pre-eminence, the hater of England and France, the preacher of imperial conquest.   There is no reference to Fichte's cosmopolitanism or republicanism.   Fichte's call for German regeneration is vitiated by a reference to the war:

We must not suppose that this prescription of austere and abstract aims implies any aversion on Fichte's part to material progress, compulsory *Kultur,* or military conquest.[5]

John Dewey's *German Philosophy and Politics* (1915) is far less a war book.   It contains three lectures delivered in February, 1915, at the University of North Carolina. Though the war is always in the background, the book is almost detached in its treatment of German Idealism in its political aspects.   The Fichte picture that emerges [6] is that of an ethical socialist who remakes the state through education, seeks freedom as a goal, and is anxious that the work of the state shall benefit humanity.   Dewey is not in sympathy with Fichte's ideas, but his discussion of them suffers chiefly because of its brevity.   This brevity did not

[3] *Op. cit.,* p. 5.
[4] *Op. cit.,* chapter 7, pp. 73-84: " Fichte on the mission of Germany."
[5] *Op. cit.,* p. 78.
[6] *Op. cit.,* pp. 68-89.

permit him to include matters essential to an understanding of Fichte. An important clue to a real comprehension of the man and his thought is thus dismissed with a single sentence.[7] There is considerable emphasis on " Prussianism," as well as the statement found in almost all Fichte literature as to the " marked difference of attitude toward the nationalistic state before and after 1806, when in the battle of Jena Germany went down to inglorious defeat." [8]

Turning to the historians, we may mention J. Holland Rose's *Nationality in Modern History* (1916). This again is a war book, though the preface states that it was in preparation long before the outbreak of the war. Here the interpretation is both more simple and more fully developed.[9] Fichte, like Schiller and so many others at the turn of the century, was a thorough-going cosmopolite and scorned the national state. Then came the disaster of Jena in which Napoleon humiliated Prussia. Fichte then discovered that cosmopolitanism was " only a fair-weather creed." This he showed in the *Reden an die deutsche Nation,* which represent a complete turn-about from cosmopolitanism to nationalism. The *Reden* were a very great influence in their day, definitely traceable in the reforms of Stein and in the Wars of Liberation. Rose had made this interpretation previously in somewhat shorter compass in the *Cambridge Modern History.*[10] It may, then, be taken as indicative of a definite trend in Fichte studies.

A more ambitious, though practically worthless, attempt in the field of historical interpretation is J. G. Legge's

[7] " In fact, his sympathies were largely French and republican." *Op. cit.,* p. 85.

[8] *Op. cit.,* p. 68.

[9] Lecture 3: " Schiller and Fichte." Lecture 7: " The German theory of the state."

[10] Vol. ix, pp. 325-328.

Rhyme and Revolution in Germany. A Study in German History, Life, Literature and Character, 1813–1850. This book appeared in 1919, is dedicated to " one of the glorious host who fought for conscience's sake and fell," and is thoroughly warlike in spirit. The only reason for mentioning it here is to produce an extreme example of the influence of the war on Fichte studies. Legge's account of Fichte [11] is based solely on the *Reden an die deutsche Nation,* especially the fourth and fifth addresses. What else there is is mere vituperation. The *Reden* are seen as " a revelation of the insanity of self-exaltation, that German megalomania which, preached as a gospel throughout a whole century, . . . was indeed to provoke the very crack of doom." [12] There is but one short sentence which suggests that Fichte was " in sympathy with pure republicanism." [13]

It would be a simple matter to expand this list of Fichte interpretations. The significant thing about them is not so much that they were wartime utterances, but rather that they represent a definite, perhaps dominant, trend in Fichte scholarship.

The reason for this lies largely in the fact that Fichte has become a man of a single book—the *Reden an die deutsche Nation.* Not literally, of course, but somewhat in the manner in which Milton was long cited as the author of *Paradise Lost* to the neglect of the Prose Works. The *Reden,* too, have been most frequently translated and most often reprinted. In fact, it has come to the point where mention of Fichte recalls the *Reden,* as the name of Calvin recalls the *Institutes,* or that of Grey the *Elegy Written in a Country Churchyard.*

[11] Book II, chapter 2: " Fichte the Apostle of Germanism."
[12] *Op. cit.,* p. 77.
[13] *Op. cit.,* p. 87.

This exclusive consideration of the *Reden* produced a one-sided interpretation of Fichte's thought. The true Fichte will be discovered only after a study and comparison of all his works. With Johnsen we ask then: "What are the facts?"

CHAPTER I

Biographical Notes on Fichte

This chapter is in no wise intended as a detailed "life" of Fichte. It is to serve merely as a searchlight to bring out such phases of his background, training, and activity as will be of help in understanding the man and his thought.

Johann Gottlieb Fichte was born in 1762 and died prematurely in 1814.[1] He was perhaps a descendant of a Swedish corporal of the army of Gustavus Adolphus who had been wounded in Germany and remained in the land of his fighting and convalescence. Fichte's parents belonged to the "common people"—a fact of great importance in his life. As a lad he showed extraordinary talents which were deserving of better opportunities than his father was able to provide for him. And the fact that he was able to repeat his pastor's sermon to Baron von Miltitz—so the story goes—won him the chance he needed. Miltitz, until his own death, was the boy's patron and sent him to the excellent Fürstenschule at Pforta. Here, however, the young student was very unhappy among the scions of the proud and wealthy nobility, and this experience, too, registered its effects upon his mind.

After further studies at Wittenberg and Leipzig, Fichte went to the famous University of Jena in 1780 to pursue

[1] The outstanding data of Fichte's life may be gathered from such volumes as Léon, *Fichte et son temps* (Paris, 1922-27); Immanuel Hermann Fichte, *J. G. Fichtes Leben und literarischer Briefwechsel*, 2 vols. (Sulzbach, 1830); Fritz Medicus, *Fichtes Leben* (Berlin, 1905); Kuno Fischer, "Fichte," in *Geschichte der neueren Philosophie*, vol. 3 (Heidelberg, 1869); the article "Fichte" in the *Encyclopædia Britannica*, etc.

studies in theology and jurisprudence. Then, after four
years of study, in order to earn his living he became a private
tutor. This life took him about to various places, at first
in Saxony, later in Switzerland and Poland. He was an
observant person, and his travels, particularly in Switzerland, also affected him.

During this early period we find him strongly influenced
by the currents of thought which agitated the day. The
world of the *Aufklärung* was opened up to him. He was
greatly impressed by Lessing and Klopstock among the Germans. He also discovered Rousseau and Montesquieu at
this time, at first in secret, for books such as these were
forbidden at the schools.[2] All this merely served to in-
tensify the " winter of his discontent " with conditions as he
found them and to fan the fires of revolt.

Philosophically, the dominant force in Fichte's life was
Spinoza's closely knit system. Not that it satisfied him—
far from it. Its determinism and fatalism fascinated him
but made him very unhappy, for at first he saw no logical
escape from it. Eventually, in 1790, he read Kant and was
thrilled with joy.[3] For Kant gave him exactly what he
longed for—freedom from Spinoza's logical prison. The
Critique of Pure Reason appeared to eliminate causality
from all but phenomena and thus to open the way to the
philosophic acceptance of the freedom of the mind. Kant's
doctrine of freedom came to Fichte as a great liberating
force. So great was the impression made upon him that
he determined to go to Königsberg and study at the " source
of all wisdom."

In 1791 he made the pilgrimage to his saint. But when
he reached the shrine, he was disappointed in several ways.

[2] H. Johnsen, *op. cit.*, pp. 10, 11.

[3] See his letters to Achelis which palpitate with happiness. *Fichtes
Leben*, vol. i, pp. 107-113.

The venerable philosopher was rather dull in class and fell far below the glorious anticipations of the young disciple. When Fichte paid a personal visit to Kant, the old man seemed cold and forbidding, wholly indifferent to the ardent worshipper. But the disciple was not to be repelled in that way. What could he do to compel recognition? An idea flashed upon him. Kant's system had not yet been applied by the master to revealed religion. He, Fichte, would supply that gap and thus gain the approbation he so eagerly sought. In a little more than five weeks (July 13 to August 18) he dashed off his first contribution to philosophy, the *Versuch einer Kritik aller Offenbarung.* This he brought to Kant. The Sage of Königsberg did not thoroughly peruse the *primum opus* of his student. He paged through it, however, and recognized it as a piece of work within the scope of his own thought. He urged the young man to have it published. He did even more than that. When young Fichte found himself without funds, Kant secured a publisher for him and thus the work saw the light of day.

But the publisher knew more than type-setting. The book appeared without a name and it omitted the introduction which asked indulgence " for an immature work of a beginner." [4] The book was reviewed in a short notice in the *Jenaer Allgemeine Literaturzeitung,* perhaps the leading literary review of the day. But this short review was sufficient to " make " the book, for it declared Kant to be the author, and this lead was followed by most reviews. It was generally believed that because of the censorship, Kant had

[4] *Werke,* vol. v, pp. 12, 13. There is considerable difference of opinion on this point. Some interpret these omissions as a shrewd publisher's trick, which was calculated to produce the precise course of events that followed. Others, among them Léon (l., 6. 141), explain the omissions by " l'inadvertance de l'éditeur." Kuno Fischer declares that there was a double title-page, one for Königsberg with Fichte's name, the other for Leipzig without it.—*Op. cit.,* 2nd edition, p. 268.

grown careful and was showing circumspection by publishing his latest work anonymously.[5]   When Fichte discovered what had happened, he was deeply concerned lest the master might think that the disciple had engineered the trick.   He was relieved of his anxiety when Kant publicly denied authorship and pointed to Fichte.   The young man's reputation was made.   Like Byron after *Childe Harold,* he awoke one morning to find himself famous.

Meanwhile the French Revolution was agitating minds everywhere.   Its liberal, anti-monarchic ideas were received with enthusiasm by some and opposed with rigor by others. In Fichte the Revolution struck a sympathetic chord, or better, set fire to a powder barrel.   He was the son of a commoner and proud of it.   What indeed was the use of kings and princes who came to power by hereditary right and cared not a fig for their " subjects " ?   After Rousseau's *Contrat Social,* was it possible to tolerate such a system? Did not the Swiss demonstrate in their state how one might get along without autocrats?   Thus his lowly origin, his reading, his experience, and his travels made Fichte a partisan of the Revolution.

When he perceived that public opinion was beginning to turn against the Revolution, he penned two furious attacks on the old order.   In the *Zurückforderung der Denkfreiheit* he used the Prussian Censorship edicts of 1788 as a text from which to denounce autocratic government.   And in the *Beiträge zur Berichtigung der Urteile des Publikums über die französische Revolution* he sought to establish an ethical basis for the right of revolution.   Both of these pamphlets appeared anonymously, but it was impossible to hide their authorship.   Fingers were pointed at Fichte from

---

[5] *Fichtes Leben,* vol. i, pp. 139-142.   Kuno Fischer points out (*op. cit.,* p. 350) that this was bad literary criticism.   Though the ideas of the *Versuch* are Kantian, its style and phraseology are utterly un-Kantian.

all sections of Germany. Good conservative monarchists trembled with fear and roared with indignation at this dangerous " democrat," this " secret Jacobin." About this time, Fichte also joined the Freemasons and possibly the Illuminati. Both of these societies were, at least in sections, champions of democratic government and were frequently attacked as revolutionary.[6] This democratic sympathy with the French Revolution is extremely important for an understanding of Fichte.

And then in 1794 the University of Jena decided to appoint the young philosopher and radical to take the place of the celebrated Reinhold. Jena was then at the height of its fame. It attracted students from all parts of Germany and from other countries. Its *Allgemeine Literaturzeitung* was very influential. Its professors were chosen for their scholarship and brilliance. And the " secret Jacobin " Fichte was now asked to join the faculty. It was an act of courage not often found in universities. To be sure, the Duke of Saxony was liberal and his minister was none other than Goethe, who, though hardly a liberal, might be trusted with the task of appointing men of distinction. So it happened that when Reinhold, the great man of Jena, was transferred to Kiel and a successor was sought to propound Kantian philosophy, none was deemed fitter for the position than the young author of the *Versuch einer Kritik aller Offenbarung.* When Fichte's name was mentioned for the position, there was strong opposition, based solely on his democratic sympathies and his attack on the old order. Anxious inquiries were made by the university authorities. Voight, the curator of the university, wrote to Hufeland:

> Ist er (Fichte) klug genug seine demokratische
> Phantasie oder Phantasterei zu mässigen?

[6] For Fichte's relationship to Freemasonry, see the Appendix.

[7] X. Léon, *op. cit.*, vol. i, p. 264.

Men have been denied positions for less than Fichte was "guilty" of. But in this case it was Goethe who stood firm and insisted on the appointment. Later he himself characterized it as "ein Entschluss der Kühnheit, ja der Verwegenheit."[8]

For the next five years (1794-1799) Fichte lectured on philosophy at Jena. By the brilliance of his lectures he speedily obscured the reputation of his great predecessor Reinhold. He wrote voluminously and lectured frequently to mixed audiences. And he did not sacrifice his democratic ideas. We find him occupied with plans for a French translation of his *Beiträge zur Berichtigung des Urteils des Publikums über die französische Revolution*. He urges the editor of the *Züricher Zeitung* to copy frequently from the *Moniteur* and the *Journal de Paris* in order that French ideas might be known more widely in other countries.[9]

Among the students he was definitely a liberal influence. Several clubs were organized under his guidance in which democratic ideas and their application were openly discussed. The Illuminati are said to have had a strong organization at the university of Jena.[10] French students came in large numbers to study there, so that we find this expression from Fichte:

> Überhaupt ist Jena, und insbesondere ich, in
> Frankreich bekannt genug.[11]

When the Duke of Weimar came on a visit to Jena he found the entire faculty servile in its attention to him. Only Fichte would not yield his "rights of man," at which the duke expressed his joy in a letter to Goethe.[12] Finally, Fichte

[8] *Fichtes Leben*, vol. i, p. 164.
[9] *Fichtes Leben*, vol. i, p. 214.
[10] Léon, *op. cit.*, vol. ii, p. 20.
[11] *Fichtes Leben*, vol. i, pp. 215 *et seq.*
[12] *Fichtes Leben*, vol. i, p. 215; Léon, *op. cit.*, vol. i, p. 276.

received some attention in the *Moniteur* as a friend of France.[13]

All of these matters invited attack by his enemies. Chief among these was the newly-founded journal *Eudaemonia* which had come to the defense of "hearth and altar." It demanded Fichte's removal from the university. But Goethe and the Duke stood firmly by their appointee and refused to yield to the clamor. Still Fichte was a marked man, deemed a danger to the home, the church, and the state.

These years were also marked by bitter controversies with the students and the student fraternities. Fichte was opposed to the fraternities and their dueling practices. He finally succeeded in getting a promise from several important fraternities that they would dissolve, if they were granted general amnesty. Since the government hesitated on this latter point, the fraternities thought Fichte was betraying them and caused him much trouble. At another time Fichte found it necessary to retire to a small town which served as a refuge after a student riot.

In 1799 the opposition came to a head. The charge of atheism was brought against him. In the *Philosophisches Journal,* of which he was an editor, an article was to appear by Forberg on the "Development of the Idea of Religion" ("Entwicklung des Begriffs der Religion"). Fichte, not wholly satisfied with the study, prefaced the article with one of his own: "*Über den Grund unsers Glaubens an eine göttliche Weltregierung*" (The Basis of our Belief in the Divine Government of the Universe). In this he declared that the terms "God" and "Moral Order of the Universe" were synonymous. This was immediately declared to be a denial of a personal god. The cry of atheism was raised and the government was called upon to take action against the dangerous professor.

---

[13] Léon, *op. cit.,* vol. i, p. 280.

Now as a matter of fact, there was nothing particularly new in Fichte's article. His doctrine might well claim Spinoza as parent, or if a more ancient and venerable sire were sought, Aristotle. If these names brought discredit as those of a Jew and a pagan Greek, there were Lessing, Heidenreich, Mueller, and many others who propounded essentially the same doctrine.[14] That of course would not prevent *Eudaemonia* and the "defenders of hearth and altar" from denouncing Fichte. It should be noted that the attack was not against an innovation or a new idea, however subversive it may have appeared. The target aimed at was far more the man Fichte, the democrat, the Jacobin, the Freemason, than any religious heresy.

The government at Weimar was again faced with a dilemma over its turbulent philosopher. The Elector of Saxony suppressed the journal and demanded that the offender be punished, lest he forbid Saxons to attend Jena. But Weimar was not willing to go beyond a rebuke for carelessness, administered by the Academic Senate at Jena. Meanwhile a miniature pamphlet war was being waged over the issue. A group of prominent writers published a joint declaration in behalf of Fichte. Fichte himself made a strong answer to the accusations in his *Appell* and *Verantwortungsschrift*. He pointed out that the basis of the attack was really political, that is, that it was directed against his democratic and Jacobin sympathies.[15]

The storm might well have blown over as on previous occasions, had not Fichte been betrayed into recklessness. On the advice of a friend, he sent a letter to Voight in which he threatened to leave, and stated that many other professors would leave with him " should he be severely reprimanded." He claimed subsequently that the letter was

[14] Léon, *op. cit.*, vol. i, p. 535.
[15] *Fichtes Leben*, vol. i, pp. 166-169.

a private and therefore a privileged communication, but it was clearly of a threatening character and was addressed to the curator of the university. No wonder that the curator communicated it to the government. Once more Goethe came into the picture. Just as he had dared all opposition and appointed Fichte in 1794, so now he was the deciding factor in dismissing the man who thought he could coerce his government with a threat. Weimar accepted Fichte's resignation. No matter that this was undoubtedly a severe blow to the university. No matter that the students protested and appealed the decision and that they went about singing: " There is only one Fichte as there is only one God." [16] No matter that Fichte himself recognized the mistake he had made and declared that the case he had postulated, i.e., a severe reprimand, did not exist. Weimar would not listen; Fichte had to leave the university.[17]

But what did Fichte mean when he threatened to leave Jena and take many other professors with him? The answer to that question throws further light on his ideas and sympathies. By the Treaty of Campo Formio in 1797, the French had obtained possession of the left bank of the Rhine, including the city of Mainz. In the letters printed in *Fichtes Leben* [18] there are several which are concerned with the revival of the University of Mainz. The plan was to gather there a great faculty which should be in sympathy with the French democratic ideas and which should teach them to young Germany. Fichte was consulted in the matter and was invited to make suggestions. For over a year negotiations proceeded. The founding of a pro-French university at Mainz was undoubtedly what Fichte had in mind when he threatened to leave Jena and take other pro-

[16] Léon, *op. cit.*, vol. i, pp. 622-626.
[17] Kuno Fischer, *op. cit.*, vol. v, p. 289; Léon, *op. cit.*, pp. 535 *et seq.*
[18] Vol. i, pp. 299 *et seq.*

fessors with him.   The project did not materialize, however, much to Fichte's disappointment.   Nor did the expected exodus of protesting sympathizers from Jena occur.   Still, the negotiations and the apparent willingness of Fichte to carry on virtually in the service of the French are significant for his outlook at that time.

The obvious place for Fichte to go in Germany, after leaving Jena, was Berlin.   At Berlin there had been many changes since the days of the Great Frederick.   But there still remained a kind of tolerance, halting though it was, and a goodly number of important literary men.   At Berlin Fichte was admitted to the circle of Schlegel and Schleiermacher, and he joined (or rejoined) a lodge of Freemasons affiliated with the Grand Orient of France.   He earned a comfortable living by lecturing and writing, and more and more he became an orator.   Already as a tutor he had showed great interest in the art of the orator.   In the Berlin period he became almost wholly the orator, and his writings, with very few exceptions, assumed the character of oratorical speeches.

When the French moved on Jena in 1806, Fichte went to Königsberg, where he taught for a season, and during one summer he also lectured at the University of Erlangen. After the defeat and humiliation of Prussia by Napoleon, Fichte returned to Berlin, where, in the winter of 1807-1808 he delivered his famous *Reden an die Deutsche Nation*.   In 1809 he became one of the founders of the University of Berlin, where also he taught for several years.   His activity in suppressing the dueling student fraternities brought new trouble on his head, so that he retired from the university. He and his wife now gave their time and energies to the fight against Napoleon.   Fichte offered himself as chaplain in the Wars of Liberation, but his services were refused. Yet he did address the troops on occasion.   His wife became a nurse. Attending to her arduous duties she was stricken with typhoid fever, and while nursing her, Fichte contracted the disease. He died January 29, 1814, only 52 years of age.[19]

From these brief biographical notes certain characteristics of Fichte appear which merit some elucidation. Fichte was a very *impulsive personality*. This is evident from many instances in his life. As a boy he ran away from school, determined never to return. He threw all his resources and energies into the task of gaining Kant's favor. His hatred of princes and autocracy is expressed in unrestrained invective. He knew no compromise. He carried his ideas to their extreme consequences. For that reason they are often unreal, theoretic, and even fantastic. He was logical to a fault, and like all consistent people he was betrayed into some strange absurdities. His impulsive nature also brought him into conflict with almost everybody with whom he came in contact intellectually. His life is filled with controversies. Kant, Schiller, Fessler, Goethe, Schlegel, Schelling, Pestalozzi are but examples of the many with whom he disagreed rather violently.

Another important characteristic of Fichte was his *democratic liberalism* which was later poured into a *socialist* mould. The son of " common people " never denied his origin. He believed in the essential value and dignity of the individual. To him, princes and priests were parasites who had no right to their privileges. From Rousseau he learned about social contracts, and this concept he carried to such lengths as virtually to make it meaningless. But it did serve to emphasize the contrast between " the people " and " the princes." When the French Revolutionaries

[19] Most biographies give January 27 as the day of death, but this has proved to be an error. See Medicus, *Fichtes Werke* (Leipzig, 1911-12), vol. i, p. clxxx.

undertook to state abstract democratic principles in the practical form of constitutions prefaced by ringing declarations of the rights of man and the citizen, when they abolished feudalism, disestablished the church, dethroned the king, and set up a republic, Fichte felt that a new era had dawned in human affairs.   Even the excesses of the Revolution could not cool his ardor.   His thought was very powerfully influenced by the ideas and the events of the French Revolution; his political philosophy was certainly derived mainly from it.

As he sympathetically observed the course of the French Revolution, Fichte coupled with his democratic idealism a socialist philosophy.   By " socialist " he meant simply the control by society, through the state, of the most important activities of the citizens.   In his earlier writings Fichte was by no means a socialist, but rather a liberal of the *laissez-faire* sort who as an individualist wished to minimize the scope and activity of the state.[20]   But subsequently, under the influence of the French Convention, he veered completely away from *laissez-faire*.   Of course, the socialism which he espoused differed in many vital points from later Marxism.[21]   It more nearly resembled Lassalle's system, and Lassalle actually acknowledged his debt to Fichte.[22]

We may note further that Fichte was *not a great scholar,* nor had he any ambition to become one.   His attitude is well expressed in a letter to his bride:

I know the profession of the scholar and I have little to learn about it.   Personally I have exceedingly little inclination to become a professional scholar.   I do not wish merely to *think,* I

[20] Nico Wallner, *Fichte als politischer Denker* (Halle, 1926), p. 271.

[21] Marianne Weber, *Fichtes Sozialismus und sein Verhältnis zur Marx'schen Doktrin* (1900).

[22] See e. g. Ferd. Lassalle, *Fichtes politisches Vermächtnis und die neueste Gegenwart* (Hamburg, 1860).

want to *act*; least of all do I want to think about the Emperor's beard.[23]

This does not mean that Fichte paid no attention to the currents of thought which flowed strongly in his day. Far from it. He read constantly and his intellectual descent is traceable from illustrious parentage, particularly German and French. In his later days he studied Spanish, Italian and Portuguese.[24]

There was, moreover, *little originality* in Fichte. With some few exceptions, his ideas were all borrowed and their sources arc readily detected. Jean Paul declared that Fichte quite erroneously " considered much that was old, as e. g. his ideas on education, love of country, as his own, and he seemed to think that he had blazed every trail over which he traveled." [25]

Finally it may be added that Fichte was *not very popular* in his day. His strong individuality, his impulsiveness, his numerous personal conflicts, served to create the impression among his contemporaries that he was an egotist. Nor was he in the least reticent as to his high personal opinion of his own philosophical contributions. He contrasted his thought with that of Kant to the latter's disadvantage. He identified *Deutschtum* with his own philosophic system. And he noted, which should not occasion surprise, that he had no friends or intimates. His unpopularity must be kept in mind for a proper appreciation of Fichte's life and work.

[23] *Fichtes Leben*, vol. i, p. 56.

[24] *Fichtes Leben*, vol. i, p. 427. I find no indication anywhere that he read English or had anything but a casual acquaintance with the great English political thinkers, except as their ideas became burning issues, as e. g. Locke and Burke. And Burke is apparently known through a German discussion (Rehberg).

[45] Körner, " Wirkungen der Reden Fichtes," in *Forschungen zur Brandenburg-Preussischen Geschichte*, vol. xl, pt. 1 (1927), p. 66.

CHAPTER II

FICHTE'S POLITICAL PHILOSOPHY

FICHTE'S political philosophy is deeply rooted in his general philosophic system. It will therefore be necessary to refer briefly to the fundamentals of his thought. Fichte was a disciple of Kant. Kant had insisted on the unity of experience, but he had not deduced the various categories from a single source. Fichte was logical and posited a single source which he found in the free spirit of man. This placed him at the very opposite pole to the materialists and rendered him the apostle of Idealism pure and undefiled. The world itself, according to Fichte, is the creation of Free Spirit, not the reverse; and Free Spirit set up an external world in order to provide a field for moral endeavor. Or to put it another way, because man is fundamentally a moral being he has found it necessary to set up an outer world; and this world is merely the stuff of moral action. God is the Moral Order of the Universe.

This is a system of ethical idealism which has its counterpart (though lacking its metaphysical basis) in Matthew Arnold's "power that makes for righteousness" and in Carlyle's "moral enthusiasm." [1]

The two fundamental concepts of Fichte's system are these: man is free; man is moral. Only as man realizes these two ideals does he live a life that is truly worthy of himself. But this cold statement of fact conveys a wholly

[1] See, e. g., Arnold, *Essays in Criticism* and Carlyle, *Sartor Resartus.*

false impression. Fichte does not generally propound his ideas with the abstruseness, the philosophic calm and detachment, of Kant. He preaches the doctrines of freedom and righteousness with the fervor of a Franciscan friar. He is an Apostle of Freedom and Morality. His purpose is not so much to convince the intellect as to stir the emotions and incite action. He is seeking to make converts who will prove the faith that is in them in their daily living. Fichte's philosophy is in reality his religion, and he clothes it not infrequently in religious terms, particularly during his later period. It is an ethical optimism which predicates that the moral order of the world will make for the final victory of the right.[2]

A corollary to the doctrine of the Moral Universe is that of Duty and Conscience. Luther's idea of the *Beruf,* the vocation, for every occupation and undertaking, and also Kant's Categorical Imperative are largely individualistic concepts. Fichte gave these ideas a wider and deeper interpretation by making them social. All social relations depend on Duty. Others had tried to find a basis for social relations in the need of association (Grotius), in the search for power (Hobbes), in usefulness (Hume), or in happiness (Leibnitz and Wolf).[3] But Fichte bases them on Duty. Only as man understands his duty and carries it out, can an ordered society come into being and perform its work.

Fichte's thought, then, moves within this orbit: Freedom =Moral Order of the Universe—Duty.

Within this orbit also moves Fichte's idea of the state. But there is an important development in his thought as to

[2] Fichte's ethical optimism has had influence on the development of modern religious ideas, particularly in Protestant thought.—See McGiffert, *The Rise of Modern Religious Ideas* (New York, 1915), p. 64.

[3] See Fritz Schneider, *Fichte als Sozialpolitiker* (Halle, 1894), p. 10. Dewey, *German Philosophy and Politics,* p. 71. Gerhard Ritter, *Luther. Gestalt und Symbol* (Munich, 1925), pp. 153-164.

the function of the state in achieving his great objectives.[4]
This development was due to nationalism and to the influence
of the French Revolution.

In his early revolutionary pamphlets, *Zurückforderung der
Denkfreiheit* and *Beiträge zur Berichtigung der Urteile,*
Fichte is hostile to the state.   He is dealing with an absolute
state whose powers are concentrated in the hands of irresponsible, hereditary princes.   Yet only a few years later, in the
Grundlage des Naturrechts, and above all in *Der Geschlossene Handelsstaat* and in the *Reden an die Deutsche Nation,*
his attitude is completely reversed.   He has cast off the
" nightwatchman theory of the state," for he now affirms the
state; the state has even become a friend.   He even sees in
the state the instrument by which his ideals may be achieved.

This fundamental change came with the development of
nationalism in Fichte's thought.[5]   As long as local patriotism or cosmopolitanism was Fichte's guiding star, he was
indifferent to the state and its organization.   More than that,
the state was either something petty which every intelligent
and cultured man might despise, or it was a tyrant, an
oppressor, which must be fought.   However, as soon as
nationalism entered Fichte's thought, all that was changed.
The state became an ally, something to champion, a powerful agent in the service of freedom.

Fichte's nationalism grew and developed under the influence of the French Revolution.   When the Revolution
was fighting the absolute and irresponsible power of hereditary kings, it tried to minimize the power of the state.   It
sought to withdraw from the state various functions, insisting that it shall " keep in its sphere," and that its sphere

----

[4] See Nico Wallner, *Fichte als politischer Denker,* chap. 2: "Frei-
heitsenthusiasmus," pp. 35-82. Dunning, *A History of Political Theories
from Rousseau to Spencer* (New York, 1920), pp. 138-141.

[5] See chap. vii.

was merely to protect each individual in his personal rights and property. In other words, the Revolution at first was liberal, *laissez faire*. But with the establishment of a democratic régime, the outbreak of foreign wars, the threat of rebellion at home, the disorganization of finance, the necessity of providing food for millions, and a host of other problems, a change took place in the attitude toward the state. No more was it a hated institution which must be regarded with fear and suspicion. It had become an instrument in the hands of the people by which they might solve all their pressing problems at home and abroad. Accordingly, more and more power was given to the state with the intention that it should become the means by which peace and freedom should be established. Thus the French Revolution while liberal in theory, was frequently socialist in practice.

And Fichte, a close observer of the Revolution, followed. He championed the right of the people to control their government. He ascribed to the state not only great political power, but he advocated placing the entire economic life of the country under its control. Finally he gave over to the state the whole sphere of education. Thus the French Revolution made the nationalist Fichte also a socialist.

In discussing Fichte's political theory, we may well leave aside his early thought and dwell on his later nationalist and socialist concepts of the state.

In Fichte's theory there is a sharp distinction between the people (*das Volk*), and the state. The people (*das Volk*), come first. But as long as there was no state there was no freedom. The exploitation of the people and the exercise of irresponsible power could go on unhindered. There was nothing to prevent it. It was for that reason that the state came into being. Its purpose was to establish and protect the freedom of the individual. This it accomplished by law.

Fichte, in contrast to Bentham, draws a sharp line of demarcation between ethics and law. Ethical principles are universally binding without distinction of place. They are the soul of the Universe expressed through a sense of Duty by the guidance of Conscience. But Law is the method which the people have chosen to guarantee freedom when organizing a state. For freedom is possible only through the law of the state.

The state came into being through a contract, a free contract of all the people among themselves. Every social relationship was based on a contract. First, there was the *Staatsbürgervertrag,* the social pact by which the state was created. But this was immediately interpreted or supplemented by the *Eigentumsvertrag,* the property contract. Fichte uses this term in a very wide sense. " It designates not merely the possession of real property, but the right of free action in the world of sense." [6] This is in turn followed by the *Schutzvertrag,* the protection contract, " by which guarantees are given that each will help the other to protect his property," that is, his freedom. And these two contracts are properly established and protected by the *Vereinigungsvertrag,* the union contract. By this the coöperation of all is assured in the great work laid out for the state. When the economic life of the people is discussed, another series of contracts makes its appearance. These are multilateral contracts between the three great economic groups: the producers, the manufacturers, and the merchants. Thus the entire life of the state is based on contracts.

The purpose of the state is the establishment and guarantee of freedom. This may be achieved in two ways: by education and by compulsion. Accordingly, the state has a Janus-like aspect. On those who are willing to be educated to be free and to respect the freedom of others, it smiles benignly;

[6] *Grundlage des Naturrechts. Werke,* vol. iii, p. 195.

on those who are not susceptible to the milder, educative form of persuasion, it frowns in righteous indignation. Fichte's preference unquestionably was for the former method. He believed that the people were educable, that they might be led to freedom. For that reason he referred so often to Pestalozzi's ideas on education, to the importance of trained and educated men in the government, to the need of schools. For that reason also he spent much time on the lecture platform doing what he could to lead and guide education.

But when education fails, compulsion, force, steps in. The state is absolute in power. Everyone of its members must be in complete subjection to it, must yield unquestioning obedience. If any member fails to do so, it is the business of the state to compel him. For the state is also *Zwangsstaat*. The individual is like a member of the body, the eye or the hand, inseparably bound up with it. He does not exist for himself. He must do what is expected of him, what is his duty. If he has not *learned* to do this willingly, he must be *compelled*. This compulsion is part of the inalienable sovereignty of the people, for it is based on the General Will, the *volonté générale*. Since the people have of their own free will made a contract by which the state came into being, they will yield absolute, but free, obedience to their creation.[7]

However, let us suppose that the individual, exercising his right of freedom, does not wish to belong to such a state. Well and good, says Fichte, let him step out of the state and merely be a member of the people (*das Volk*). He loses

[7] Fichte was a great admirer of Machiavelli. He sees the Florentine's contribution to the idea of the state in this, that the power of the state must be absolute and be enforced without stint. He also adduces Machiavelli's example in the interest of freedom by citing him against censorship. See *Machiavelli als Schriftsteller, Nachgelassene Werke*, vol. iii, p. 401 *et seq.*

greatly thereby, but he has a perfect right to exercise his prerogative.   This privilege was later revoked and membership in the state became a duty.[8]

It will bear repetition that this absolute, compulsive power of the state is established as a guarantee of freedom.   At first this seems a rather poor joke, and not a few have declared that in reality it was the death-knell of freedom.[9] For Fichte's state appears to clamp a worse despotism on the people than the one from which he sets out to deliver them.   The answer to this apparent anomaly lies in the contrast between liberty and equality, between Liberalism and Socialism.   In other words, it is the difference in the methods and tactics employed to achieve freedom and human well-being.   A strong emphasis on " liberty " will frequently destroy " equality," and *vice versa.*[10]

The state has other business than the guarantee of freedom.   It has a civilizing mission; it furthers *Kultur,* civilization.   What *Kultur* is for Fichte is difficult to define.   It appears to be merely formal will, the will for creating values. What the object of this will is to be, what values are desirable and are to be created, in which scale these values appear: these are matters which Fichte does not discuss.[11] *Kultur* arises from the people.   Another famous German said many years later: " As for the masses, may the Devil and Statistics take them ! "   But Nietzsche's idea is the very opposite of Fichte's.   For Fichte the masses are capable of assimilating *Kultur.*   If only they are properly led, they are the carriers of *Kultur.*   It is the business of the state to

---

[8] These are matters of pure theory.   It is hard to understand how they could be carried out in practice.

[9] E. g. Wallner, *op. cit.,* p. 127.

[10] See Schevill, *The Making of Modern Germany* (Chicago, 1916), pp. 164-167.

[11] Wallner, *op. cit.,* pp. 58, 59.

further *Kultur* among the people. In this way the culture of each national state will acquire national characteristics.

The chief means for accomplishing this is education, *Erziehung.* Therefore the state has also an educational mission. Consonant with his earlier point of view, Fichte at first designated the family as the best educational agent. But as his concept of the state and its functions changed, he assigned education to the state, because the family had proved itself incompetent for the task.

The state, furthermore, has definite economic duties. Most great political thinkers have discovered that their political and legal discussions of the state automatically involve economic corollaries. The two run together in the thought of Hume, Ferguson, Leibnitz, Chr. Wolff, Montesquieu, and others.[12] Fichte, too, realized early that civil liberty and political freedom were empty words when divorced from economics. That is why he pronounced Rousseau's idyllic state of nature a silly notion. The state of nature is chaos, it is synonymous with ruthless exploitation and economic inequality. Largely for this reason the state has come into being. The state of Reason as contrasted with the state of Nature is concerned with bringing about and establishing economic order and security.

The " son of the soil " again shows his descent, the quarry whence he was hewn. For Fichte the basis of all economy is agriculture, or in a larger sense, the production of raw materials.[13] From this basis a series of economic contracts are arranged between the various groups : producers, manufacturers, and merchants, so that each group works for the welfare of the other, as well as its own. In this way the property contract receives a specific meaning.[14] It implies

---

[12] Schneider, *Fichte als Sozialpolitiker,* p. 5.

[13] *Grundlage des Naturrechts, Werke,* vol. iii, p. 217 *et seq.*

[14] *Ibid.,* p. 210 *et seq.*

the right to work and to live. It is the business of the state to guarantee these rights to all. Only in this way are economic freedom and security established. But this duty of the state involves its complete control of the entire economic life. It means State Socialism. And though the term "socialism" does not appear till 1833,[15] Fichte must be put down as one of the first modern socialists, though by no means of the Marxian type.[16]

Despite its wide functions, there are fields wholly outside of the jurisdiction and sphere of action of the state. These are chiefly the teaching of Religion, Science (*Wissenschaft*), and Morals. The state does all in its power to encourage these, but it does not prescribe their content or teach them. To some extent this is only an earlier attitude of Fichte. In his later teaching the state virtually takes these over as well, though the terms must be defined widely to include them.

Something must also be added here as to the government of the state. Is it to be an absolute monarchy or a fully-developed democracy? Fichte's answer to this may sound strange, after his sympathies are known. For he declares that any form of government is good except a pure democracy.[17] Governmental power in a state must always be delegated. Ultimately the power, all power, rests with the people. They have agreed freely to create the state and theirs is the final determination as to what is to be done. But that does not by any means imply that they shall be governed by a pure democracy. A pure democracy may be possible in a very small community, but even there it is irksome to call together all the people whenever any matters are to be decided. Furthermore, if the community as a whole is to exercise the

[15] Kirkup, *History of Socialism* (5th edition, London, 1920), p. 3.

[16] Marianne Weber, *Fichtes Sozialismus und sein Verhältnis zur Marx'-schen Doktrin* (1900).

[17] *Grundlage des Naturrechts, Werke*, vol. iii, p. 286.

executive power there would in reality be no authority. Anarchy would result and the very purpose of the State would be frustrated.

Such a constitution, the democratic in the real sense of the word, would be the most insecure imaginable. One would have to fear not only irresponsible exploitation, as though there were no state, but also from time to time the blind fury of the excited mob working injustice in the name of the law.[18]

Anything, then, but a pure democracy. There is no escape from the delegation of power. For government is nothing if not clothed with authority, and it can function only through a strong executive.

That does not mean, at the other extreme, that the government should take the form of an irresponsible despotism. No matter how great the authority of the government, it is always responsible government. It must abide by the constitution. It must remain within the law. For that reason the people must establish the proper checks and balances, so that it does not get out of hand. The two forms of government, then, which are ruled out are pure democracy and irresponsible despotism.[19]

Anything between these two extremes is possible and permissible: a limited democracy, a pure or mixed aristocracy or aristodemocracy, an hereditary aristocracy, or even an hereditary monarchy. The essential thing is that the government shall be strong enough to exercise authority, while at the same time it is responsible to the people.

The government is elected by the people. It is assumed that all citizens have the right to vote. Woman suffrage is not mentioned and obviously not thought of. But all elections in these fundamental matters must be unanimous. To

[18] *Grundlage des Naturrechts, Werke*, vol. iii, p. 158.
[19] *Grundlage des Naturrechts, Werke*, vol. iii, p. 160.

try to determine these basic things by a majority vote is to coerce the minority. The minority must agree to the election and thus make it unanimous. But the election of the proper government presupposes a high degree of intelligence, which is not found among many peoples. Wherefore other methods of securing a government may be used. A government may be *appointed* by the educated classes from among themselves. Or governmental office may be a matter of *inheritance* within a family—always presupposing its competence. These two latter methods are preferable to election, since they guarantee more intelligent selection.[20]

Fichte's government has great authority. Lest it abuse its powers it must be competent and public-spirited. It must be made up of trained administrators who are philosophers. Fichte is really resurrecting Plato's " philosopher-kings " or Klopstock's *Gelehrtenrepublik*." [21] The importance of this type of government is better understood when we recall that one of its chief functions is education. The dual function of educational institution and *Zwangsstaat* demands philosopher-rulers competent to do their work properly and wise enough not to abuse their authority.

Fichte knew Montesquieu's argument for the separation of powers within the state. He scorned the idea.[22] The state has a constitution, adopted by the people. This constitution is not merely the fundamental law of the state; it is also a virtually all-sufficient law code. Law-making, legislation, is conceived of as an act of the people really synonymous with constitution-making. All that is needed, then, in a government is an executive which will interpret, administer, and enforce the law.

[20] *Grundlage des Naturrechts, Werke*, vol. iii, p. 288.

[21] Wallner, *op. cit.*, p. 247; Dunning, *op. cit.*, p. 146.

[22] See e. g. his review of Kant's *Zum ewigen Frieden, Werke*, vol. viii, pp. 427-436. Also his *System der Rechtslehre, Nachgelassene Werke*, vol. iii, p. 631.

The strong, almost absolute, executive, the *pouvoir exécutif,* is the real governing body. It combines with its administrative and executive functions judicial power. It is utterly useless to try to separate these two activities. They cannot in reality be kept apart without crippling the government. The executive cannot be checked by interpretations of the law which hinder the exercise of its authority. The judiciary must not be emasculated by an executive which refuses to carry out its decisions. Sound government demands that the executive and judicial functions of the state be vested in one body.[23]

But there is the possibility that this executive may prove dangerous and usurp power for its own ends, despite its careful selection. There must be a check, there must be supervision of some kind. For this purpose the Ephors are created. Elected by the people, or specially selected, this board of supervisors never relaxes its vigilance over the executive. It insists upon the rights of the people as laid down in the constitution. Freedom and security must be guaranteed to all. Injustice, maladministration, usurpation of power for selfish purposes must be prevented. The Ephors have no right to make laws or to govern. Theirs is solely a *veto power.* But this veto power is absolute. It nullifies the acts of the executive, and the executive must respect the veto.[24] Another check on the executive is pitiless publicity for all its acts.[25] In this way the people will be able to judge whether the executive is true to its trust or not.

But suppose both the executive and the Ephors fail; suppose both are consumed by selfishness, betray their trust, and seek power for themselves. In that case the people re-

[23] *Grundlage des Naturrechts, Werke,* vol. iii, p. 289.

[24] *Grundlage des Naturrechts, Werke,* vol. iii, pp. 163-172.

[25] *Grundlage des Naturrechts, Werke,* vol. iii, p. 168: " die höchste Publicität."

sume their ultimate authority by rebellion, by revolution.　It is really a false use of the word to call this a " rebellion," for the people cannot rebel against themselves.　They merely take the situation in hand, because their representatives have failed them.　It would be far better if this could be done by calling together the entire community in order to settle the difficulties and re-establish its rights.　But when that fails the people are fully within their province when they overthrow the government and establish another which will remain within the constitution.

On the whole, however, Fichte was not much concerned with these extreme possibilities.　He chose the executive with great care from the educated, the trained, the wise, the responsible, the public-spirited.　In all likelihood, he believed, these would prove true to their trust.　He selected his Ephors with almost greater care.　These would act as a check on even the slightest tendency toward unfaithfulness on the part of the executive.　Thus while the background of the picture is action by the people, the foreground is a faithful executive and a body of Ephors who are deserving of all trust and confidence.[26]

About all of this there is one astounding fact.　There is no representative body, no parliament.　This is all the more

[26] The institution of the Ephors is borrowed from Sparta.　They appear in another form as the " tribunes of the people " among the Romans. They are found in the writings of Plato, Calvin, Althusius, and Rousseau.　In the American colonies the " ephors " were introduced in Pennsylvania (1776) and Vermont (1777) as the " Council of Censors." " These latter were charged with the duty of inquiring whether the constitution had been preserved inviolate.　The Censors were abolished in Pennsylvania in 1790; in Vermont they existed until 1870; having met thirteen times and having ten times proposed constitutional changes."— Raymond G. Gettell, *History of Political Thought* (New York, 1924), p. 318.　Dunning, *op. cit.*, p. 148, suggests that the idea of the Ephors and the need for them are shown " in the constitution-making influence of the British Parliament and the Supreme Court of the United States."

surprising when we recall Fichte's enthusiasm for the French Revolution, and his close acquaintance with Rousseau and Montesquieu. The omission assumes additional importance when it is noted that Kant has no need for a parliament either. To be sure, the executive and the Ephors assume most of the functions of the parliament. Nevertheless the omission sheds significant light on the political thought of Germany at the turn of the century.[27]

[27] See *Fichtes Werke*, vol. iii, *Einleitung*, pp. xxx *et seq.*

CHAPTER III

Jacobinism

1793

We shall now turn our attention to the works of Fichte pertinent to this study, examine their origin, summarize their ideas, and thus get a fuller and more detailed picture of Fichte's political thought and his contribution to the doctrine of nationalism. In doing this, attention will be focused constantly on all expressions of nationalism and cosmopolitanism, so that at the close we may have a fairly complete record of all important pronouncements of Fichte on the subject. This examination will proceed chronologically.

Über den rechten Gebrauch der Regeln der Dicht- und Redekunst. October 5, 1780

This is Fichte's valedictory in Schul-Pforta. It was published for the first time by Maximilian Runze in *Neue Fichte-Funde aus der Heimat und Schweiz* (Gotha, 1919). The only thing worthy of remark for our present purposes about this juvenile oration is its praise of " heroes." The young orator declared that the development of mankind has proceeded, as far as the records show, through the instrumentality of heroes. At first these were men of great physical strength, heroes in war, heroes of a people not yet cultured. But later these heroes discovered that they could exercise a far greater influence by becoming heroes of a different type. Thus new conditions produced new heroes and through them mankind grew out of a state of barbarism into one of culture.[1]

The same idea appears later, especially in the *Grundzüge des gegenwärtigen Zeitalters*, Lecture 3.[2]

Zufällige Gedanken in einer schlaflosen Nacht. 1788

These notes were written in July, 1788, before Fichte's departure for Switzerland. Fichte was visiting his home in order to ease the strained relations which had arisen between him and his parents. While there, sleeplessness overtook him and he jotted down this sketch. It covers about three pages and was intended to be the first draft of a more detailed work. It is interesting also as first evidence of the deep and abiding influence of Pestalozzi on Fichte's thought. *Zufällige Gedanken* is a denunciation of the superstitions and corruptions of the privileged upper classes, the ignorance of the people, and the injustice of society. Fichte bemoans his times. He finds everything in utter decay: government by the princes, justice, religion, learning, the arts, conscience, agriculture, morals, education. Such deplorable conditions will make impossible all *patriotism* and *humanitarianism*. It is high time for someone to write a picture of the times which he might call the " Letters of Marquis de St. to his friend Viscount X. in Paris from the newly discovered southern Polar lands. Translation from the French."

We may note four important characteristics of these *Gedanken*. First, they show the " commoner " Fichte in rebellion against the injustice and corruption of autocratic

---

[1] *Op. cit.*, p. 36 *et seq.*

[2] Carlyle's *Heroes and Hero Worship* is somewhat dependent on Fichte. The relationship has been studied in Margaret Storrs, *The Relation of Carlyle to Kant and Fichte* (Bryn Mawr, 1929). Nietzsche's "hero" philosophy in relation to Fichte is discussed in Charles Andler, *Nietzsche, sa Vie et sa Pensée*, vol. i, *Les précurseurs de Nietzsche* (Paris, 1920), chap. 5, " Fichte," pp. 99-100.

government.   Secondly, his expression takes form under the influence of French ideas, no doubt, the *Lettres Persanes* of Montesquieu.   Thirdly, we see already the moral preacher who was subsequently to develop his system in detail. Finally, we must underline mentally Fichte's regret that patriotism cannot flourish under the circumstances he decries.   And this patriotism is intimately linked with humanitarianism—perhaps the same as cosmopolitanism.

Zurückforderung der Denkfreiheit von den Fürsten Europens, die sie bisher unterdrückten. Heliopolis, im letzten Jahre der Finsternis.   (1793)

Noctem peccatis, et fraudibus objice nubem

This powerful pamphlet was written against the Prussian Censorship edicts of 1788.   The Prussian king Frederick William III was a Rosicrucian and readily influenced by his surroundings, especially by Pastor Woellner.   Woellner secured from the king an edict on religion and another on censorship.[3]   Both were reactionary.   Two inquisitorial bodies were put in charge of the enforcement.   In 1789 the Censorship forbade all reading and speaking about the French Revolution.   All journals were in danger of suppression.   This act brought forth a huge protest which centered in the pamphlet *Freimüthige Betrachtungen über das Edikt die Religionverfassung in den preussischen Staaten betreffend* (Frankfurt und Leipzig, 1788).   Fichte was no Prussian, but from his point of view he thought it not amiss to enter the controversy.   Strangely enough, he believed that the Censorship edicts were wise and he praised them highly. In three separate pronouncements he placed himself at the side of the Prussian king and asked the Prussians to recognize the wisdom of his actions.[4]

[3] Léon, *op. cit.*, vol. i, p. 117 *et seq.*

[4] Léon, *op. cit.*, vol. i, pp. 117-131, 159-163.   Léon prints the gist of

But there was much for Fichte to learn. The Censorship was, as is usually the case, very stupid. It did not know its friends and depended wholly on its irresponsible power. So it happened that it refused a visa to Fichte's *Versuch einer Kritik aller Offenbarung.* Fichte had planned to base his reputation on that work and was anxious to have it printed in Prussia. Besides it had the approval of Kant. But the Censorship denied permission to publish in Prussia and the *Versuch* was published elsewhere. Then Kant's *Religion innerhalb der Grenzen der blossen Vernunft* failed to find favor with the Censor. The *Berliner Wochenschrift* was also suppressed. And now Fichte rose in arms.

The result was a revolutionary pamphlet. The Censorship was destroying Fichte's hope of orderly progress. With the free circulation of ideas progress was possible. But the complete suppression as then practiced made revolution the only hope. Still Fichte did not propose to wave the red flag in the face of the authorities. This was to be an appeal to the princes for the abolition of the edicts. Accordingly he blamed the clerics and the councillors of the princes for the situation as it was and asked that the princes remedy it. The indictment is so good an illustration of Fichte's enthusiasm for freedom that several passages will bear citation. It should be added that though the pamphlet appeared anonymously, its authorship was immediately ascribed to Fichte, who was henceforth considered a dangerous Jacobin.

these documents in an appendix. They are: 1. *Zuruf an die Bewohner Preussens.* 2. *Ideen zur Dedikation an Preussens gereifte Bewohner. An denjenigen Teil des Publikums, der noch unparteiisch urteilen kann.* 3. *Vorrede.* These documents are remarkable for their inordinate praise of the king of Prussia and for the fact that Fichte twice calls himself a "foreigner" in them. Writers like Fichte's son, I. H. Fichte, and Noack have tried to interpret these astonishing productions as irony, but there does not appear to be the slightest justification in the text for such an interpretation.

In the Introduction Fichte plays with the idea of revolution. He says:

(The constitutions of states are changed) in two ways: either through sudden violence or through gradual, slow, but certain progress. Through violent revolution and overthrow a people may advance further in a half-century than in ten others. But this half-century is also miserable and troublesome and it may also carry a people back into the barbarism of the last millennium. The history of the world adduces examples of both. Violent revolutions are always a daring risk of mankind. If they succeed, the victory is well worth the agony the world has suffered; if they fail, mankind has only gone through misery to greater misery. Far more certain is gradual progress to greater enlightenment and thus to the improvement of the constitution.[5]

Wherefore he appeals for freedom of thought and open discussion:

No, ye people, surrender all, everything, only not the freedom of thought. Give up your sons to the mad battle, to slaughter men who have never insulted them, or let them be devoured by plagues, or let the pestilence come to your peaceful habitations as booty of war; take away the last crumb of bread from your starving child and give it to the dog of the royal favorite; surrender, give up everything. Only this heaven-born palladium of humanity, this guarantee that you have still another future than to suffer, endure and be crushed—only that retain! [6]

But, of course, this fierce champion of freedom is overlooking entirely the reason for the action of the princes. The people are ignorant—as sheep; the princes must lead them—as shepherds. Everything is done for the well-being and happiness of the people. To this Fichte replies:

We do not know what is for our happiness. If the Prince

5 *Werke*, vol. vi, p. 5.
6 *Werke*, vol. vi, p. 7.

knows and if he is there for the purpose of leading us to happiness, we must follow the leader with closed eyes. He does with us whatever is his pleasure, and should we address a question to him, he assures us on his word that this is necessary for our happiness. He puts the rope around the neck of humanity and says: Be quiet! It's all for your good.

Just so the executioner of the Inquisition said to Don Carlos while occupied in the same way. How strange that people of different trades should meet thus!

No, Prince, you are not our God. From Him we expect happiness. From you we expect the protection of our rights. We do not ask you to be kind to us. We demand justice of you![7]

The Introduction left no doubt as to Fichte's purpose. The pamphlet proper begins with this blast:

Ye peoples, the times of barbarism are past. Then you were told in the name of God that you were herds of cattle whom God had placed on the earth that you might serve a dozen sons of God in carrying their burdens, being slaves and maid-servants to their comforts, and finally to be slaughtered for them.[8]

For man is not a chattel which can be bought and sold, inherited and given away as a gift. Man is free; he has certain inalienable rights. Neither society nor the state can take these rights from him. For how did the authority of government originate?

The Prince has all his rights by transfer from society. But society cannot transfer any rights to him which it does not possess. The question which we are about to examine: whether the Prince has any right to limit our freedom of thought, resolves itself into this: Can the state have such a right?[9]

[7] *Werke*, vol. vi, p. 9.

[8] *Werke*, vol. vi, p. 10.

[9] *Werke*, vol. vi, p. 13.

To this question he enters a decisive " No." He finds occasion to insert the remark:

It is indecent for thinking men to crawl at the foot of a throne in order to beg permission to become footstools of kings.[10]

But the Princes offer an objection. They are not opposed to freedom of speech; far from it. They are merely trying to prevent the free circulation of poison which will most certainly prove fatal to many people. For this action of kindness they deserve thanks rather than reproach. Yes, but what is poisonous and what is wholesome food? In other words: What is truth?

You speak of objective truth. And what is that? O ye wise sophists of Despotism who are never embarrassed for a definition! It is, you say, the agreement of our concept of things with the things themselves. The sense of your demand is therefore — I blush for you as I say it — when my conception of a thing really agrees with the thing itself, then I may promulgate it; if not, I must keep it to myself.[11]

He ridicules the idea and continues:

Truth in reality, then, is what you wish to be true; false is whatever you wish to be false.—Why you wish it to be so is not a question for us to ask, nor even for you. Your will as such is the sole criterion of truth. Just as our gold and silver receive value through your minting, so also our ideas.[12]

And then with precious sarcasm:

May an uninitiated eye dare to cast a glance into the mysteries of state administration, for which deep wisdom must be necessary, since, as is generally known, only the wisest and best of

[10] *Werke*, vol. vi, p. 15.
[11] *Werke*, vol. vi, p. 18.
[12] *Werke*, vol. vi, p. 21.

men are ever placed at the helm: then permit me a few remarks. If I do not flatter myself overmuch, I see some of the advantages which you have in mind. It is easy for you to subjugate the body of man. You can place his feet in the stocks and his hands in chains. You can even, through threat of starvation and death, prevent him from saying what he ought not to say. But you cannot be everywhere with your stocks and fetters and executioners, nor can your spies be omnipresent. Besides, such a troublesome government would leave you no time whatever for pleasures and amusements. Therefore you must search for means to subjugate him more certainly and reliably, so that, though free from stocks and fetters, he does not even breathe in a manner other than you permit.

I admire in history, which is your favorite study,[13] the wisdom of a number of the first Christian emperors. With every change of government there was also a change of truth. Even during a single administration, if it happened to extend over a longer period, truth had to be changed several times. You have caught the spirit of this wisdom, but you have—pardon the beginner in your exalted art, should he be wrong—not yet penetrated far enough. . . .

Imitate, O Princes, these worthy models fully. Reject today what you commanded as a matter of faith yesterday, that the people may never lose sight of the fact that your will alone is the source of truth. You have, for example, willed a bit too long that One shall equal Three. The people have believed you, and, I am sorry to say, have so accustomed themselves to the idea that for some time now they deny that the credit for this belongs to you, and imagine that they have discovered this themselves. Avenge your honor. Command now that One shall be One—of course, not because this contradicts the other, but simply because you willed it.[14]

Then he turns on the clerics who have fostered the laws of

[13] This is aimed at Burke and his argument of " historical rights " and " historic continuity " used in denouncing the French Revolution.

[14] *Werke*, vol. vi, pp. 21-22.

censorship for the support of their Books of Confession.
He asserts that it is morally impossible to give up freedom
of thought.

You are frightened by the audacity of my conclusions, ye friends
and servants of ancient darkness, for people like you are easily
frightened. You hope that I will at least add a cautious " in so
far as," to leave open a back door for your religious oath, your
Symbolic Books, etc. If I had such a door I should not open it
for your pleasure. It is only because you have always been
handled with silk gloves and been shown extreme deference, because your bleeding sores, which are most dangerous to you,
have been overlooked, because attempts were made to wash your
Negro-black skin without touching you with water: therefore
you have become so noisy. From now on you will gradually
have to accustom yourselves to see the truth in all its nakedness.

But I will not leave you without comfort. What do you fear
from those unknown lands which lie beyond your horizon and
to which you shall never come? Ask the people who travel in
them whether there is such great danger of being swallowed
alive by Moral Giants or by Sceptic Sea Monsters. See these
brave circumnavigators of the world, morally at least as sound as
you, walking about among you. Why are you so terribly afraid
of the sudden enlightenment which would appear if everyone
were permitted to spread the light as much as he is able? The
human mind advances only step by step, from light to light. In
your day you will still be able to hobble along. You will retain
your small select group and the conviction of your own great
merits. And if really now and then a great step forward is
made through a revolution in the sciences, even that need not
trouble you. Even if the dawn does break for others, you and
your beloved wards for whom you are so anxious, will be able
to keep your bleary eyes in comfortable darkness. Yes, take
comfort, it will even be darker about you. You ought to know
this from experience. Is there not far greater confusion in your
heads since the great enlightenment has come to knowledge these
last ten years? [15]

[15] *Werke*, vol. vi, p. 24.

Having thus disposed of the clerics, Fichte returns to the Princes.

And now permit me to return again to you, O Princes. You prophesy nameless misery if unlimited freedom of thought should prevail. It is only for our best that you take it from us and deprive us of it, as children lose a dangerous toy. You have journalists, writing by your instruction, who paint in colors of fire the disorders which occur when opinions differ and minds become excited. You point to a gentle people sunk to the viciousness of cannibals, thirsting for blood and not for tears, more eager for executions than for the theater, jubilantly exhibiting the torn-off parts of the bodies of their fellows still bleeding and smoking, children finding more enjoyment in bloody heads than at play.

We will not remind you of even more bloody festivals which Despotism and Fanaticism, the usual allies, have given to this people; we will not remind you that this is not the result of the freedom of thought, but of the long previous mental slavery; we will not tell you that it is nowhere more quiet than in the grave. We will concede everything; we will throw ourselves full of remorse into your arms and beg you with tears to protect us at your fatherly bosom from all dangers that threaten—as soon as you answer another most humble and respectful question.

O ye Princes, who, as we hear out of your own mouths, are appointed to watch over the happiness of the nations as benevolent guardian angels; ye Princes, who—you have assured us of that so often—have only this one purpose of your kindly care, why, under your august supervision, do the floods still destroy our fields and cyclones our acres? Why do flames still leap out of the ground and devour our homes? Why do the sword and plagues wipe out thousands of your beloved children? Command the hurricane to be silent; then you may command the storm of our indignation. Send rain to our parched fields and have the sun to shine when we ask it: then deliver to us also blessed truth. You are silent? You cannot do these things? . . . Princes, that you are not our tormenting spirits is good.

That you want to be our gods, is not good. Why will you not make up your minds to come down to us and become the First among Equals? You will never succeed in governing the world. And you know it.[16]

With this he couples a strong plea and admonition:

Prince, you have no right to suppress our freedom of thought. And what you have no right to do you must never do, even if round about you the world should perish and you and your people should be buried under its ruins. For the ruins of the world, for yourself, and for us under the ruins, He will provide who gave to us those rights which you respected.[17]

Over our freedom of thought, therefore, you have no right, ye Princes: no decision over that which is true or false; no right to determine the object of our researches or to set limits to them; no right to hinder us from spreading the results, whether they be true or false, to whomever we please.[18]

And finally learn to know your real enemies, the only offenders against majesty, the only violators of your sacred rights and persons. They are such as advise you to leave your people in blindness and ignorance, to spread new falsehoods among them and uphold the old ones, to hinder all free researches and to forbid them. They look upon your realms as realms of darkness which simply cannot survive in the light.[19]

This fierce attack is not merely the outburst of an angry writer suffering under censorship. It is part, and a most important part, of Fichte's system of thought. Freedom to him is as much a law of the universe as are hurricanes and fire. If the princes cannot command the storm and give orders to the sun, how can they presume to violate the Moral Order of life by abridging Freedom? As a battle-cry in the

[16] *Werke*, vol. vi, p. 26.
[17] *Werke*, vol. vi, p. 28.
[18] *Werke*, vol. vi, p. 29.
[19] *Werke*, vol. vi, p. 34.

seemingly never-ending warfare against censorship and suppression this neglected classic is worthy of a place beside Milton's *Areopagitica* and John Stuart Mill's *On Liberty*.

Next to the emphasis on freedom may be placed the idea of the social compact as an explanation and a basis of government. Here Rousseau's influence is plainly visible. Governments exist by virtue of the rights transferred to them, and their authority is limited by that transfer. The form of government, monarchic or democratic, is not discussed. Insofar as Fichte is opposing the encroachments of government on the liberty of the individual, his attitude in this pamphlet is wholly liberal, not socialist or anarchist. The right of revolution is not questioned. Revolutions occur as last desperate acts of a downtrodden and enraged people. As such they may very well be a step forward. In short, this pamphlet shows Fichte as a militant liberal.

Beitrag zur Berichtigung der Urteile des Publikums über die französische Revolution. 1793

When the news of the French Revolution first reached Germany it was greeted with rejoicing.[20] This need not cause surprise. Voices of freedom had been heard frequently in Germany throughout the eighteenth century. Salzmann's revolutionary novel *Carl von Carlsberg* enjoyed wide popularity. Just before the outbreak of the Revolution young Schiller wrote revolutionary dramas. In *Die Räuber* he attacked society in general; in *Die Verschwörung des Fiesco zu Genua* he presented a republican tragedy; in *Kabale und Liebe* he denounced all class distinctions.

After 1789 the voices of revolution and freedom increased and multiplied. Klopstock wished for a hundred voices to celebrate the liberty of Gaul. His disciple, von Stolberg,

---

[20] Léon, *op. cit.*, vol. i, chap. 5: "Fichte et la Révolution Française," p. 166 *et seq.*; Johnsen, *Das Staatsideal J. G. Fichtes*, p. 23 *et seq.*

joined him. Wieland noted the great events day by day
and rejoiced that he had lived to see the time when the most
civilized nation of Europe showed how a government might
be based on the Rights of Man and on Reason. Körner
saw the revolution as an act of God. Schiller even planned
to set up his residence in France. Goethe, too, not suspect
of any revolutionary ardor, was caught in the current, and
in a memorable passage in *Hermann und Dorothea*[21] he
celebrated the Revolution. Herder evinced great sympathy
for the defenders of France and hostility to the emigrés and
to the Coalition against France. Among the historians the
Revolution found friends in von Mueller, Archenholtz,
Schlösser, and others. The theatre reflected the same
enthusiasm.

After a year there was still no reaction. On the first
anniversary of Bastille Day a great public celebration was
held at Hamburg at which Klopstock recited two odes. The
universities harbored and even fostered revolutionary clubs
and associations which celebrated the happenings beyond the
Rhine and sang revolutionary songs. The venerable Kant,
who had taken his daily walk in Königsberg with such regu-
larity that according to the ancient story clocks were
regulated by his appearance, now wrought utter confusion
among the clock-setting gentry by changing his daily itiner-
ary in order to learn the latest news from France.

Among the jurists of Prussia, F. Klein wrote a justification of the Decrees of August 4 under the title *Freiheit und
Eigentum* (1790). Brandes defended the Revolution in
his *Politische Betrachtungen über die französische Revolution*. Friedrich Schulz wrote a favorable *Geschichte der
grossen Revolution in Frankreich*. Wilhelm von Humboldt,
in his *Ideen über Staatsverfassung durch die neue französische Revolution veranlasst*, though critical of the Revolution, yet saw it as a salutary influence.

[21] In Klio: das Zeitalter.

Then followed the reaction. Burke's *Reflections on the Revolution in France* appeared in 1790. Burke became the prophet of the Counter-Revolution and his book became its bible.[22] Essentially he was a conservative, a defender of the propertied and governing classes. His *Reflections* are best characterized by his own words from another work:[23] " No passion so effectually robs the mind of all its powers of acting and reasoning as fear." Add to that Lord Morley's terse comment: " The fact is that Burke did not know enough of the subject about which he was writing." Nonetheless his " bitter and petulant criticism," in which the writings of Rousseau are stigmatized as " blurred shreds of paper about the rights of man " and the Declaration of Rights becomes a " digest of anarchy," had a powerful influence. It raised a panic among all the propertied classes of Europe.

The immediate occasion for Burke's pamphlet was Price's comparison of the French Revolution with the English Revolution of the seventeenth century. Burke entered the lists against Price. He denied the analogy between the two revolutions. The English Revolution was made by the Stuarts who had violated the traditions of England. In overthrowing the Stuarts the English had merely gone back to principles as old as Magna Carta. But the French were doing no such thing. They were ranting about abstract metaphysical principles which had no existence in fact. Natural rights, social compacts, and other unrealities were purely destructive and would lead to disaster. Historic continuity is an essential condition for the collective life of a people. This argument was wedded to fierce abuse of the

[22] See Gettell, *History of Political Thought*, pp. 306-308; De Ruggiero, *European Liberalism* (London, 1927), pp. 78-82; G. R. Stirling Taylor, *Modern English Statesmen* (New York, 1921), pp. 165-209.

[23] *The Origin of our Ideas of the Sublime and the Beautiful*, part ii, sec. 2 (London, 1913), p. 88.

French revolutionary leaders and a romantic recollection of the unhappy Marie Antoinette.

Burke's alarum was immediately reechoed all over Europe. In Germany Wilhelm Rehberg, Geheimrat of the Hanoverian Chancellory, wrote his *Untersuchungen über die französische Revolution* (1793) following the trail blazed by Burke. He found occasion for a mild criticism of the French *noblesse* and clergy, while his denunciation of the Revolution was unrestrained. The Revolution, he declared, stood for the abolition of God and king. There was no justification for the change of the constitution or for economic expropriation. This was the signal for Fichte's counter-attack.

Fichte's defense of the French Revolution appeared anonymously. "What my name is, need not trouble the reader; the matter that counts here is not the trustworthiness or untrustworthiness of a testimony, but the importance or unimportance of the reasons which must here be weighed." [24] Part I was sent out as an experiment, and he watched the effects carefully. When it caught fire, Part II was written.

His purpose is stated in the Introduction: the desire to provoke thought and create discussion. Revolutions against despotism can be prevented only by instructing the people thoroughly as to its rights and duties. For that reason it is encouraging to note that the daily conversations of the people are filled with such topics as freedom and equality, the sanctity of contracts, the basis and limits of the authority of a king, etc. From all of this truth will emerge, if only the people are not afraid of the truth and if they are not too lazy to think. He adds a note "concerning the careful use of this book" which, in a footnote, he begs the reader not to overlook. He is not inciting to revolution or calling for the overthrow of existing governments. He urges patience for the present. He takes refuge in an exalted idealism: " Be

[24] *Werke*, vol. vi, p. 45.

just, ye peoples, and your princes will not be able to bear it that they alone are unjust." [25]

Then he turns on Rehberg. How shall we judge revolutions? How determine whether a people has the right to overthrow its form of government and set up another? Fichte divides the question into two parts: the rightfulness and the wisdom of revolution.[26] It is the first with which he is chiefly concerned. Rehberg had attempted to set up history and experience as judges and thus to condemn all revolutions. But Fichte at once deposes them. History describes the past, but prescribes no law for the future. Therefore history can be no guide. In fact every empirical criterion is useless, for opinions and judgments are constantly changing.

Twenty years ago we believed unseeded cucumbers to be unwholesome, and today we believe seeded cucumbers to be so.[27] Do we not know that in Constantinople such things are generally held to be true which in Rome are generally believed false? That several centuries back in Wittenberg and Geneva the same things were generally held to be true which today in the very same places are considered dangerous errors? [28]

Again, when we carry any problem back far enough we arrive at a point where there is no experience to guide us. Furthermore, the empirical answer to any question will always depend on the interests you wish to protect, the groups you desire to shield. Ask the princes, for instance, whether the people have the right to change their government. Their answer will be an immediate No—because they interpret history by their interests.

[25] *Werke*, vol. vi, p. 45.

[26] *Werke*, vol. vi, pp. 48-79.

[27] *Werke*, vol. vi, p. 51.

[28] *Ibid.*, p. 53.

It is really difficult to control one's gall-bladder or diaphragm, depending on which is more sensitive, when listening to the declamations of our experts and specialists against the application of the first principles of Reason, as well as the violent attacks of our empiricists against our philosophers.[29]

There is then no answer to these questions in experience, in history, in empiricism. The solution derived from such sources is temporary, applicable only to a certain time and to certain groups. If a permanent, an eternal, answer is desired, it must be sought elsewhere. And that source is Reason, the highest law of Nature. And what do we learn from Reason? That the basis of life is the Moral Sense, and this moral basis demands the freedom of the individual. No man is a slave or another's property. Nor does the state own man or have absolute power over him. He belongs to himself; he is free.

Man lives in society and in a state. Does this signify that he has voluntarily relinquished his rights? By no means. The state was brought into being through a social compact of free individuals with each other. They transferred certain rights to the state, but among these was not their freedom. This is inalienable. In order to explain the matter further Fichte draws four concentric circles which bound the various rights of man.[30] The outermost and widest circle is the right of conscience; the next, the right of natural law; then, the rights of contracts in general; finally the civil contract. The right of the state, and therefore of princes, is limited to the smallest of these circles. Should the state attempt to abridge freedom it is reaching over into the fourth circle, the right of conscience, where it has no authority whatever. The state was established by contract between man and man, not between the state and

[29] *Werke*, vol. vi, p. 68.
[30] *Werke*, vol. vi, p. 133 *et seq.*

man.   If at any time the people wish to change the form of
the government, it is their privilege to do so.

This right of change is inalienable.   Even if all would
make a contract with all to surrender this privilege, they
could not do so.   Nor is it a proper argument that the
people owe so much to the state in positive values and in
wise and kindly guidance that they ought to forego this right
of change.   Is it true that the people owe the very existence
of property, of education, and of culture to the state?
Fichte denies this.[13]   Property, he holds, is merely the right
to work a field, raw materials, etc., to the exclusion of others.
Education is the field of the parents and of society.   Culture
is not furthered by the state.   Thus the supposed benefits
derived from the state and the gratitude due it fade away
into thin air.

What form should the government take?   Rehberg insisted that monarchies must remain, for their abolition
would make for confusion, civil war, the *bellum omnium
contra omnes,* or subjugation by foreign powers.   But, says
Fichte, is that worse than the absolute, irresponsible power
of kings?   Have absolute monarchies ever furthered freedom?

If you wish to rule you must first enslave the mind of man; if
this depends on your every whim, the rest will follow with ease.
Unlimited freedom of thought cannot exist side by side with unlimited monarchy.[32]

There is one glorious exception, Frederick the Great of
Prussia, who worked to make his people free.   All others
believed that it was necessary to fetter the minds and spirits
of their people in order to govern.   Not Frederick.

[31] *Werke*, vol. vi, pp. 117-148.
[32] *Werke*, vol. vi, p. 99.

That saves your honor in the judgment of posterity, immortal
Frederick, raises you out of the class of crushing despots, and
places you in the honorable line of those who educated their
people to freedom. . . . You wanted the mind of your people
free; thus you had to wish them free, too, and if they had seemed
ripe for freedom to you, you would have given them that for
which your often hard rule was a preparatory discipline.[33]

This section closes with a remarkable apostrophe:

Jesus and Luther, holy protecting spirits of freedom, who in the
days of your humiliation worked with giant strength at the fetters of mankind and smashed them in many places, look down
from your exalted sphere on your descendants and rejoice over
the seed that has grown and the harvest bowing to the wind.
Soon the third, who completed your work, who burst the last and
strongest fetters of mankind, though perhaps neither he nor
mankind knew it, will be gathered to you. We shall weep after
him. You will give him joyfully the place in your company prepared for him, and the age which will understand and portray
him will be grateful to you.[34]

In discussing the state Fichte distinguishes sharply between it and society (*Gesellschaft*). If a man does not
approve of the state and its laws, which he has helped to
create by contract, he may leave the state and be merely a
member of society. Then he may make a contract with
others for a new state. If this group remains within the
physical borders of the old state, there is created a state
within a state. This might appear as a *reductio ad ab-
surdum* of the whole theory, but Fichte supports this concept
with another important argument. States within states are
not unusual. In the present organization of the state various examples of this may be seen, chief of which are the

[33] *Werke*, vol. vi, p. 99.
[34] *Werke*, vol. vi, pp. 104-105.

Jews, the Military, the Nobility, the Church.[35] What is dangerous is not the mere existence of these smaller states, but the fact that they are opposing their interests to those of the people.

This leads Fichte to a long and rather repetitious discussion of the classes within the state. Rehberg had found historic justification for the favored classes. Fichte set out to destroy this claim. Part II is devoted entirely to this argument.

What of the Nobility?[36] There is no justification anywhere for hereditary nobility with great powers and large landholdings. The noble class arose through feudalism. The early Germans had no hereditary nobility. All were free, and leadership went to the most able. This carries Fichte into a lengthy " historical " examination of early Germanic history and the age of feudalism. The only nobility which would justify its existence is a nobility of mind and merit. Instead the nobles have many privileges without corresponding duties and services. By what right? It is high time that a new contract were made with this group. They are by no means the best minds. Not even that " shameless defender of nobility " [Rehberg] had dared to claim that. Look into the public service, the offices of the court, the military service, where the nobility is found, and the calibre of this group will be evident at once.

And what about the Church?[37] The visible church is a true society based on a contract. But no church has the right to demand obedience through the use of force. Everyone has the right to renounce the church. Church and state should be separate. The state has no right to interfere with or dictate to the church, nor should there be an alliance

[35] *Werke*, vol. vi, pp. 149-154.
[36] *Werke*, vol. vi, pp. 157-244.
[37] *Werke*, vol. vi, pp. 244-286.

between the two, by which on the one hand the state will compel people into the church and on the other the church will bless the oppressions of the state in the name of God. Such an alliance would be monstrous and opposed to freedom.

What about the property of the church? The church came into possession of its earthly wealth through a contract or exchange. The donor exchanged his worldly goods for the heavenly promises of the church. Now suppose that he, as one party to the contract, or his heirs, cares no longer about the heavenly promises? Then he may demand the return of his worldly goods. The state should not prevent him in this effort. Quite the contrary. Should the individual not be able to retrieve what is his, the state may take it in the name of all. If any so chooses he may let mercy and leniency prevail and not demand the return of his property and goods. But as for the right to ask it back, there cannot be the least doubt about it for any who renounce the church.

Thus we come to the end of Fichte's first problem: the rightfulness of revolution. His pamphlet is a juridical justification of revolution coupled with a denunciation of absolute monarchy and feudal and clerical privileges. The second question as to the wisdom of revolution is discussed but meagerly.[38] In the main he confines himself to answering objections against the possibility of establishing another form of government which would give greater rights to the people. He insists that the people must be trusted and that they will learn to govern. For " man can do what he should do; and if he says: I cannot, he merely does not want to." [39]

Summarizing, we find that in this pamphlet Fichte occupies essentially the same position as in the previous one. It

[38] *Werke*, vol. vi, pp. 61-73.
[39] *Werke*, vol. vi, p. 73.

differs only in greater detail and elaboration. There is the same emphasis on the inalienable right of freedom, the social compact, the denunciation of feudal privileges among nobility and clergy. There is also the same liberal attitude toward the state, that is, that it should function in a severely limited sphere. In the distinct denial of any connection between the state and property rights, education and culture, the pamphlet differs markedly from Fichte's later writings. On the other hand, in the statement that absolute monarchy cannot exist with freedom of thought, it marks a step in advance of the earlier pamphlet on the Censorship. But these two pamphlets written about the same time are animated by the same general attitude and are identical in their political philosophy. The theory of property and ownership and the justification of expropriation are the first indication that Fichte is thinking not merely in political terms, but that he senses the economic realities which lie back of politics.

Though issued anonymously there was not the least doubt among contemporaries as to the authorship of this pamphlet. The ensuing denunciation of Fichte as a Jacobin and a revolutionary almost prevented his appointment at the University of Jena. The attack was led by *Eudaemonia,* a journal whose program was the defense of " the throne and the altar." In its prospectus it announced:

The saddest events have recently occurred; and these events cannot have escaped the attention of a single statesman. For the public spirit of the German people has been attracted to ideas which threaten the immediate ruin of religion, the throne, the fundamental constitution of the Empire: atheism and blasphemy against God, hatred for the princes, open derision of all authorities, wild desire for revolution, partly provoked, partly strengthened by the cry for revolution from the pen of writers and from the mouth of orators. . . . A rapid glance into the literary history of France will suffice to show that the French Revolution was prepared by literary men.   That is exactly what is happening in Germany and it is not difficult to draw the necessary conclusions.[40]

Fichte defended himself against these attacks and heeded the warnings of friends and the admonitions of the Weimar government to be more circumspect.   In other moods he threatened to write Part III if he were not permitted freedom of expression.   The pamphlet was translated into French under Fichte's direction.

[40] Copies of *Eudaemonia* are very rare.   Léon is the first to find that journal and use it.   See Léon, *op. cit.*, vol. i, p. 302 *et seq.*: "La campagne de l'Eudaemonia."

CHAPTER IV

SOCIALISM AND THE DAWN OF NATIONALISM

1794-1806

Einige Vorlesungen über die Bestimmung des Gelehrten. 1794

IN 1794 Fichte's activity as professor of philosophy at the university of Jena began. Besides his regular academic lectures he devoted much time to student organizations. Among others the society of " Free Men," [1] was founded, and Fichte accepted the position of patron. The stated purpose of this group was " the search and dissemination of the truth " (*die Wahrheit zu erforschen und zu verbreiten*). But the last three words (of the German text) were stricken out by the Academic Senate on the ground that they were revolutionary. The society held regular meetings at which such topics as the nature of the state, the limit of its powers, the duty of the citizen, the legitimacy of war, crime and punishment, and similar political and social problems were discussed. Fichte attended the meetings, addressed the society frequently, and was a friendly mentor to the group of kindred minds.

But there were others not belonging to the society whose lives he was eager to influence. For that reason he hit upon the plan of delivering " practical " or popular (as opposed to his theoretical, philosophical) lectures to all who would attend. He endeavored to find time and place for these during the week, but soon discovered that the difficulties were insuperable. Accordingly he determined to give the

---

[1] Léon, *op. cit.*, vol. i, p. 318 *et seq.*

lectures on Sunday morning at the very hour when church services were being held. There was opposition from many quarters, particularly from the church and from the " defenders of the altar and the throne." But Fichte prevailed. He was given an auditorium in the university and his lectures were attended by great numbers of students and faculty members.

The first series of " practical " lectures was called the *Vocation of the Scholar*.[2] It consisted of five addresses and dealt with matters on which he had already expressed himself in writing. The purpose of life, he declared, was to seek a complete harmony with man's reasonable, ethical nature. He developed the ideas of society and the state, their origin and the difference between them; he denounced the artificial and hereditary differences of classes and privileged groups. In one lecture he declared that " the scholar has the supreme supervision of the real progress of mankind in general and the continual development of this progress." [3] Scholars are the teachers of humanity. They operate by persuading free men, not by force and compulsion; their guidance is accepted from conviction. In the final lecture he took issue with Rousseau's idea that the advance of civilization has been a curse to man. Rousseau's error consisted in looking at everything from the point of view of the individual. But man does not live alone, and this purely individualistic interpretation is unbalanced, one-sided. Man lives in society, and on further examination it will be found that social life has developed culture, for the real purpose of society is the development of culture.

Two important items must be noticed in these lectures. The first is the great emphasis on education and the rôle of the scholar. This idea was destined to receive more and

[2] *Werke*, vol. vi, pp. 291-346.
[3] *Werke*, vol. vi, p. 328.

greater emphasis until finally it was embodied in the classic statement in the *Reden an die deutsche Nation.* The other is the gradual veering away from the liberal individualism which he had hitherto championed. It is true that his criticism of the state and the privileged classes still has the old ring, but there is the new note of the importance of man's life in society and the growth of culture by such life. Here is the beginning of a positive social philosophy. It is not yet the state (as later), but society which assumes first importance. However, even this is distinctly a step away from his previous individualism toward a social interpretation of life. This idea was to receive its fullest development in *Der Geschlossene Handelsstaat,* though with important modifications.

Grundlage des Naturrechts. 1796-1797

It is significant that this treatise in general is positive in form and constructive in character and not largely denunciatory as were the pamphlets of 1793. Not that the spirit of 1793 is entirely absent—far from it. But Fichte is now endeavoring to accept the state; more than that, the state is assuming an important place in his notions of the life of the individual and the institutions of society.

Fichte is seeking the basis of natural rights " according to the principles of science " (*nach Principien der Wissenschaftslehre*). Accordingly he prefaces his discussion with a long and rather abstract disquisition in which he emphasizes the importance of the outer world (*die Sinnenwelt*) and of the society of men. This is in sharp contrast to his earlier emphasis on the individual.

We begin, then, with the fact of an existing society. Under such circumstances it is essential for peaceful and harmonious life that each individual voluntarily restrict his personal freedom of action, lest great harm ensue through selfishness. But in natural society there is no guarantee that all will do this. In fact it is more than likely that there will be violations of freedom and personal property.[4] For that reason there must be law to regulate and guarantee freedom and property. And if necessary (and it is necessary) this law must be coercive (*Zwangsrecht*).[5]

Coercive law must be administered by the state. The state exists through a civil contract of all its members voluntarily entered into.[6] Its purpose is seen in the three important contracts which are included in the civil compact: the property contract, by which property rights are established and secured; the protection contract, by which the property contract is enforced; and the union contract, which assures and protects the first two.[7]

The government of the state may be anything except an absolute monarchy or an absolute democracy. Both are tyrannies. Power must be delegated to a government which may be a limited monarchy, an oligarchy, or a limited democracy. Officials may be elected by the people or appointed by the " best minds." The rulers are best chosen from the educated classes. These have the ability both to rule and to feel the responsibility placed upon them. In this government the executive and the judiciary are united. Government is not so much by legislation as by decree or by a constitution which embodies all necessary laws.

The executive is the real power of the state. It has a double check. First the Ephors, chosen from the educated, have an absolute veto power over all acts of the executive. If both the executive and the Ephors fail in their trust and attempt to assume power for selfish reasons, the people them-

[4] *Werke*, vol. iii, pp. 120-126.
[5] *Werke*, vol. iii, pp. 137-149.
[6] *Werke*, vol. iii, pp. 191-209.
[7] *Werke*, vol. iii, pp. 195-204.

selves step in, either by a great assembly which will re-establish government as it ought to be, or by a rebellion, really a wrong name for the assumption of power by those to whom it belongs.[8]

A long discussion of marriage is also included. It is important to note that education is made the right and the duty of parents.[9]

Finally Fichte adds a section on the law of nations and the rights of world citizenship. In this he adumbrates a kind of league of nations and world court through which eternal peace is established.[10]

The problem of international relations arises when a dispute between the citizens of two states is to be settled. Both states are independent, each seeks to protect its citizen and to have him judged according to its own laws. In order to avoid constant conflicts, diplomatic officials were exchanged and thus a kind of mutual supervision arose. But at some time there may be a state which does not recognize the independence and integrity of other states. In the past the answer of the other states has always been war.

There is a better way to bring such a state to order, namely, the organization of a league of nations. This league will be effective chiefly through an international court and through public opinion. All disputes are submitted to the court for judgment, and if the court is unfair, its injustice will be obvious to all and it will condemn itself. It will soon learn to be scrupulously just. The appeal to arms still remains, in which case all members of the league will send an army against the aggressor. Since this will happen but seldom, it is not necessary for the league to have its own army. An executive *ad hoc* army will save much expense

[8] *Werke*, vol. iii, p. 160 *et seq.*

[9] *Werke*, vol. iii, pp. 359-368.

[10] *Werke*, vol. iii, pp. 369-385.

and will also serve the purpose better. Under this system injustice will still be possible, but it will not occur frequently. As the league spreads and does its work, eternal peace will be ushered in.

It is evident that this treatise represents a great development in Fichte's political thought. The state is not a thing to be feared or to be got rid of. It has become of supreme importance. Through it alone freedom and security and property in the widest sense are created and established. For that reason it has great powers, powers even of coercion over the violators of the rights of others. Those powers are reflected in centralized organization. There are checks on its government through the Ephors and through the possibility of "direct action" by the people. But the great power of the state is a definite fact.

On the other hand there remain strong reminders of Fichte's earlier position. The purpose of the state is personal freedom. The right of revolution is recognized. Certain spheres are still denied to the state, notably education. Thus the development begun in the addresses of 1794 goes on.

Des Herausgebers des Philosophischen Journals Gerichtliche Verantwortungsschriften gegen die Anklage des Atheismus. 1799

This document grew out of the accusation of atheism against Fichte in 1799. It was preceded by the *Appellation an das Publikum*, a purely religious argument addressed to a wider circle. An appeal is here made to the Prorektor of the university. After demonstrating the ridiculous character of the charge leveled against him, Fichte proceeds to analyze the basis of the accusation and the animus behind it. He finds it in the fact that he is a danger to the state.

I am to them a democrat, a Jacobin; that's the real reason. Of such one believes every abomination without proof. Against such a one it is impossible to commit an injustice. Even if in this case he has not deserved what has happened to him, he has deserved it another time. In any case it serves him right.[11]

It is not my atheism which they are endeavoring to punish, but my democratic principles. The former has merely given them a convenient occasion.

I am called a democrat. And what is that? Is it one who declares the democratic form of government to be the only rightful one and who advocates its introduction? It seems to me that if one did this even in a monarchic state only in learned treatises, the refutation of this opinion, if it be wrong, might be left to other scholars. As long as one does not commit an overt act in order to overthrow the existing government and to install the form of government advocated, I cannot understand how one's opinion can be brought before the tribunal of government, for only actions belong there." [12]

He goes on to declare that the hatred against him is due to his earlier revolutionary writings which were the " indiscretions of a young man," justifiable enough because of the arbitrary despotism of government, but which after maturer thought he would have modified considerably. His later writings are proof of that, as well as his record in the last five years. Nor is he at present an instigator of revolution. He has no time for that. He is busy elaborating a system of speculative philosophy. Besides he really loves his country.

I hereby declare with the greatest frankness that there is today no country in Europe in which I would rather live than in Germany. There is also no position anywhere in which I would sooner be than the one in which I am at present. I need nothing but quiet and peace around me and personal security; every-

[11] *Werke*, vol. v, p. 286.
[12] *Ibidem*, p. 287.

thing else I shall get for myself.   These two boons the German
laws have thus far granted me.[13]

Thus the man without a country of the revolutionary
pamphlets of 1793 has become, in his own fashion, a patriot.

Philosophie der Maurerei (Briefe an Konstant).   1800

Fichte joined the Freemasons in Zurich in 1793.   When
he was dismissed from Jena and went to Berlin he found
friends there among the members of the fraternity.   On
April 11, 1800 he joined one of the Berlin Masonic lodges,
that of *Pythagoras zum flammenden Stern* which was
affiliated with the Royal York of the Grand Orient.[14]
Known as an orator he was asked to address the lodge,
which he did on April 13 and 27, 1800.   These two lectures
constitute the work now under examination.[15]

Fichte's purpose in addressing the Freemasons was to

[13] *Werke*, vol. v, p. 295.

[14] On this Masonic connection see the Appendix.

[15] The literary history of these two lectures is very curious.   Fichte
gave the manuscript to Johann Karl Christian Fischer, a high official of
the Grand Orient.   Fischer published it for the first time in the
*Eleusinien des 19. Jahrhunderts oder Resultate vereinigter Denker über
Philosophie und Geschichte der Maurerei* (Berlin, 1802-1803, 2 vols.).
But Fischer was an astonishing editor.   He took great liberties with
Fichte's manuscript.   First of all he converted them into letters supposedly addressed to a non-Mason (Konstant) and he gave these the title
Briefe an Konstant.   Not content with that he introduced into the text
short introductory and summarizing paragraphs to round out the letter
form.   And to crown this work he interpolated a long discourse of his
own in defense of Free-masonry, calling it Letter No. 2.   The editing of
these lectures in order to restore the original text is a difficult task.
Since the original manuscript is lost, it is partly guess-work.   Fichte's
Werke edited by his son did not include the lectures.   The edition here
used is by Wilhelm Flitner (Leipzig, 1923).   Flitner has not reprinted
Letter No. 2 and has endeavored to restore the original text by bracketing
what seem to him the additions of Fischer.   He has also prefaced the
edition with an excellent Introduction.   For a textual criticism and history see this Introduction, p. cccxix *et seq.*

win them for other than purely social purposes. He was endeavoring to make the order a potent force in the regeneration of mankind. Therefore he pointed out to his hearers that on the one hand the Freemasons were attracting their members from all classes: rulers, princes, nobles, scholars, artists, merchants; and on the other hand from all confessions: Catholics, Lutherans, and Calvinists. Nevertheless they were being persecuted in many countries, and two popes had denounced them.[16] Under these circumstances it was time for the members to ask themselves the real purpose of the organization. He proceeded to answer this question himself.

The sole purpose of human existence on earth is neither heaven nor hell, but our human nature, which we carry about with us, and its highest development.[17]

This must be the purpose of every truly wise man. But at present it is being vitiated by the existence of classes and of an education which fits people to be members of their class rather than of humanity. This makes for one-sidedness and is deplorable.

This evil can be remedied by special societies whose purpose it is to further the highest development of mankind. Society in the larger sense of the word cannot do this. It should, however, encourage the efforts of the smaller groups. And the ideal to be striven for is the creation of a man, harmonious, resting in himself, clear in thought, artless in virtue, who knows himself to be free and " who in faith already lives in a better world." [18] And this must be the real purpose of the Freemasons: an educational order seeking the highest human development.

[16] *Philosophie der Maurerei*, p. 6.
[17] *Op. cit.*, p. 11.
[18] *Op. cit.*, pp. 25-26.

In his second address Fichte develops the ideal in detail. The goal of education must be the creation of a single human congregation whose members act through ethical motives. And alongside of such a spiritual union must stand a political organization, in which all mankind is really gathered in a single state.   Not that a world state is to be organized, but all states are to be based on Reason and their relations among each other will thereby virtually constitute a single unit.[19]

This leads to a discussion of the political activities of the Freemasons.   Is their goal to be cosmopolitanism and a lofty ignoring of the state or have they a part to take in the work of the individual state?   Fichte's answer must be cited in full:

Now do not believe that the completely educated man is thereby withdrawn from his state and devoted to a lazy, cold cosmopolitanism.   On the contrary he becomes the most complete and useful citizen.—Even as in religion, his thought is always with the eternal, but his entire strength is with earthly things: so in regard to politics (*Rechtlichkeit*) his mind is always on the whole, while his entire strength is given to his state, his city, his office, his special locality on earth. *In his mind love of country and cosmopolitanism are intimately united,* and both stand in a very definite relationship. *Love of country is his activity, cosmopolitanism is his thought; the former is the outer manifestation, the latter the inner spirit of the manifestation, the invisible in the visible.*

For even as a religion, dear Konstant, which would exist in the abstract, is vain and perverse and even ridiculous: even so a cosmopolitanism which would exist in the abstract and exclude patriotism is vain and useless and absurd.   "The individual, concrete thing is nothing," says the cosmopolite; " I think of, am concerned about and live for the Whole; this shall be improved and peace and order shall be spread over this."   Well

[19] *Op. cit.*, p. 33.

and good; but tell me first how you propose to approach this Whole with the beneficent ideas and purposes which you harbor for it. Do you propose to benefit it in general and in wholesale fashion? Is the Whole anything different from the individual parts united in thought? Can the Whole in any way be improved if the individual parts are not improved? Take pains first of all to better yourself and then better your neighbor to the right and to the left. Then I believe that the Whole has also gained because one or two or three individuals in it have improved.

The Freemason understands this; and therefore his cosmopolitanism expresses itself through the greatest activity for the specific place where he finds himself.[20]

As for the religion of the Freemason Fichte declares:

He shall not be a Jew or an uncircumcised proselyte, or a Roman, or an Arab, who has religion, but he shall simply be any man who has religion.[21]

These lectures are the first clear statement of Fichte's conception of the relationship between cosmopolitanism and patriotism. Cosmopolitanism by itself is " lazy," " cold," and therefore " vain, useless, and absurd." Patriotism by itself is narrow and selfish. In the truly educated man the two must be found together.

Again we must note the emphasis on education. In the pamphlet on the French Revolution education was left with the parents or ascribed to society as a whole. Here the parents are not mentioned. By inference the task of education is denied to society as a whole and to the state. It is placed in the care of " special societies " whose whole energies are given to it.

[20] *Op. cit.*, pp. 45-46. Italics Fichte's.
[21] *Op. cit.*, p. 40.

Der Geschlossene Handelsstaat. 1800

This study had its origin in a practical problem.   At the close of the eighteenth century the idea of free trade was steadily making headway.   Mercantilism was open to criticisms which appealed especially to the politically powerful Woellner.   Gradually Prussia began to relinquish mercantilism for free trade.   In 1786 Minister Werder issued an order abolishing mercantilism.   This sudden action led to an economic crisis the solution of which was eagerly sought. Prussian experience apparently demonstrated that neither mercantilism nor free trade brought economic welfare.   It was to this concrete problem that Fichte addressed himself in this pamphlet.[22]

Fichte considered his study of the *Closed Commercial State* to be one of his best and most thoughtful works.   It certainly marks a great departure from his earlier thought on the state.   In the introduction we come upon this statement which is a revealing self-criticism:

There has been abundant criticism in our day of the idea that the state is the unrestricted guardian of mankind in all its affairs, that it should make them happy, rich, healthy, religious, virtuous, and God willing, lead them to eternal bliss.   On the other hand, I believe, the duties and the privileges of the state have been too closely circumscribed.[23]

This faulty notion Fichte wishes to correct.   He had worked his way through politics to economics.   The importance of the state he now saw in its relation to the life and work, the security and well-being of all citizens.   In securing these highly desirable conditions he ascribed to the state a dominant rôle.   And to show his hope and desire that his plan might find practical realization, he addressed the work

[22] Léon, *op. cit.*, vol. ii, p. 58 *et seq.*

[23] *Werke*, vol. iii, p. 399.

to the Prussian Minister, Herr von Struensee.   At the same
time, he expressed his doubts as to the willingness or possibility that his age would adopt the remedy he proposed.[24]

Fichte began with the idea of work.   The purpose of all
work, he stated, is joy, not slavery.   Work must give satis-
faction and rest, it must build personality.

It is not merely a pious wish of mankind, but its persistent and
rightful demand and its destiny that it may rule over nature as
easily, as freely and as dominatingly as Nature itself permits,
and thus live in a truly human way on earth.   Man should work;
but not as a beast of burden which falls asleep under its load and
after the most necessary rest of its exhausted strength is again
roused to resume its burden.   He shall work without fear, with
joy and pleasure.   He shall find enough time for himself to
raise his spirit and his eye to the heavens, which he was made to
behold.   He shall not eat with his beast of burden; but his meat
shall differ from the provender of his cattle and his home from
the stall as much as his body differs from that of the beast.   This
is his right, simply because he is a man.[25]

How can this be achieved?   The answer is, by the economic contract.   By this contract each gets his place in life
and his sphere of activity, and thus economic security and
freedom are established.   It is the business of the state to
see to the enforcement of this contract.

This leads on to a discussion of the meaning of property.
What is property?   It is not the possession of things, but
rather the right to work, the right to a sphere of activity to
the exclusion of others.   It may be the right to work a
certain area of land, or the right to fashion certain raw
materials into finished products through the various
handicrafts.

[24] *Werke*, vol. iii, pp. 389-394.
[25] *Werke*, vol. iii, p. 422 *et seq.*

What this property, this work, shall be, is to be determined by the state through a very careful, detailed, and efficient division of labor.   The state divides the workers into three classes:

1. the producers, such as farmers, foresters, gardeners, etc.;

2. the artisans, such as mechanics, workers of raw materials, etc.; and

3. the merchants, that is, the distributors of goods.

Multi-lateral contracts are made among the three groups. The producers contract to deliver to the artisans what they need; and the artisans in like manner to the merchants.   The purpose of each group is to help, not to hinder, the others. Therefore the arrangement may be counted on to succeed.

Besides the three classes of workers, there are three other groups, the officials of the state, the teachers, and the army. These groups, whose work is just as important as that of the " workers," are paid by the state.   The only tax levied is for the pay of these necessary groups.   Their pay is to be equal to that of the workers.

In this scheme of things there are many difficulties to cope with.   Good and bad years must be taken into account. Fichte tried to equalize them by a standardized average year. Credits are granted to regions suffering in one year, but they must repay them in good years.

A fundamental difficulty is the existence of money based on gold and silver values.   The power of this money must be got rid of.   Fichte thought to achieve this by three great operations:

1. the state establishes and fixes the value of all things and their price;

2. the state creates a purely national money (*Landgeld*) in contrast to world money (*Weltgeld*);

3. the state isolates itself commercially by gradual steps

until it is wholly independent of foreign commerce and economically self-sufficient.

To establish a sound basis for value Fichte sought something that constituted an absolute necessity. Gold and silver were artificial bases, useful because serviceable and convenient in exchange. Value ought not to be determined in that way. Value ought to rest in the first place on use, in the second place on the possibility of exchange. He chose as the basic value a bushel of grain. All values were to be stated and measured by this standard. Thus he got rid of the gold standard and substituted the grain standard.

Next, he provided for a means of exchange. Obviously it was impossible to do business or even barter with bushels of grain. The convenience of coined money was not to be denied. Fichte therefore established a system of grain-money. A bushel of grain might be exchanged for a one-grain note, and all other values were to be regulated by this standard. This money was not to be gold or silver, but something else. It should be made in a manner difficult to imitate. What it was made of should not concern the people very much, as long as it passed in trade for the indicated value. He suggested that paper or leather be used. This new money should be purely national in value. A world money would also be in existence but the state should remove it from circulation and have complete control over it. Since everybody would be secure and free through the economic contracts, there would be no need for saving except for old age, sickness, and the rearing of children. Money would merely serve the convenience of the people. Nor would there be need of hoarding; the free circulation of money would be assured by the state and no stringencies need be feared.

This system was given its cornerstone with the closing of the frontiers commercially. The state would develop within

its boundaries all that it needed. At first it would be necessary to carry on a considerable foreign trade, but this would
be exclusively a state monopoly. Scholars, artisans, tech-
nicians, and manufacturers would be brought in from other
countries to develop such industries as were considered necessary or desirable and which were not to be found there.
Machines and inventions would also be introduced; likewise
all needed domestic animals, plants, and raw products.
Some products which were climatically impossible of culti-
vation would continue to be imported by the government.
Otherwise the state would be sealed hermetically against
foreign commerce. Thus a state which would be virtually
self-sufficient would gradually emerge.

This would have important results in domestic and foreign
arrangements of states. Each state should have natural
boundaries, for certain portions of the earth are ordained to
be states by their physical constitution—by rivers, mountains, productivity, etc. By a system of exchange each
existing state should establish its *natural frontiers*.

These indications of Nature as to what shall remain together
and what shall be separate are meant when the new political
theory speaks of *natural frontiers* of countries. This consideration is of far greater importance and to be taken far more
seriously than is customary. And this is not solely to be referred to frontiers secure in the military sense, but far more in
the sense of economic independence and self-sufficiency.[26]

Natural boundaries eliminate the need of conquest and
thus get rid of war. The closed commercial state with-
draws entirely from international politics; it has no interest
in them and nothing to gain from them. In domestic
policy it would ensure the virtual abolition of armies and
armaments.

[26] *Werke*, vol. iii, p. 480.

The only contacts which a closed state should maintain with the rest of the world are intellectual. Travel is not permitted to all; in fact it is forbidden to the generality. Only scholars may travel, because through them intellectual contacts are established and preserved.

If a man should find this arrangement irksome, he may emigrate. At first, while the experiment is being organized there probably will be considerable emigration. But once the plan is in full working order, conditions will be so idyllic that none will think of leaving. On the contrary, the country will receive many visitors, who will be eager to see this happy land. Visitors will receive the national money in exchange for world-money while they are in the country. On the other hand, world money will again be turned over to those who travel abroad.

Great happiness will result from this arrangement. The people will live in security, freedom and prosperity. They will be relieved from the evils which often make life so intolerable, especially from burdensome taxation and military duties. Taxation will be light and wars improbable. Crime will be greatly reduced, since there will be no poverty or insecurity of life. Great influence will be exerted on the people's habits and customs. A strong and sharply differentiated national character will be developed; the people will be attached to their fatherland with a fervent love; a high conception of national honor will be fostered.

It is worth noting that Fichte's thought is closely related to the economic experiences and ideas of the French Revolutionaries. The relative self-sufficiency of France, the virtual nationalization of French economy during the troublesome years, the decree of the maximum, the state control of grain, the *assignats* as national money: all these are reflected in this new politico-economic theory. Likewise the doctrine of the national frontiers, though very old in France, was again proclaimed by Danton, for whom France had her frontiers *marquées par la Nature*," [27] and by Grégoire, who had "consulted the archives of Nature" in the matter.[28] Fichte's definition of property was probably derived from Babeuf, but Robespierre spoke the same language.

Fichte's Utopian work was soon forgotten. It had no immediate influence. Most histories of socialism pass it over without notice. But thirty years after it was written it bore fruit abundantly. Lassalle's *Theory of the State,* which holds "that we must widen our notion of the state so as to believe that the state is the institution in which the whole virtue of humanity should be realized," [29] is obviously Fichtean.

Grundzüge des Gegenwärtigen Zeitalters. 1804-1805

This series of lectures is an attack on the "aberrations" of Romanticism.[30] When Fichte came to Berlin he was warmly received in the circle of the Romanticists, including such men as Schelling, the two Schlegels, Novalis, Tieck, and Schleiermacher. German Romanticism was deeply indebted to Fichte; its ideas were based on Fichtean conceptions. At the same time Fichte borrowed from the Romanticists. For Fichte was both the last of the Rationalists and the first of the Romanticists.[31]

---

[27] Léon, *op. cit.*, p. 19.

[28] Madelin, *The French Revolution* (English translation, New York, 1923), p. 314.

[29] Cited in Kirkup, *History of Socialism*, p. 101. Here, too, should be mentioned Lassalle's *Fichtes politisches Vermächtnis und die neueste Gegenwart* (1860), a commentary on Fichte's notes to the Prussian king's *Aufruf an mein Volk*. This shows very definitely Fichte's influence on Lassalle.

[30] Léon, *op. cit.*, vol. ii, pp. 394-463.

[31] Haym, *Die romantische Schule* (Berlin, 1914), pp. 13 *et seq.*, 248-260, 293-299.

But the relations between the two were by no means harmonious. There was always the personal element which, in Fichte's case, wrecked many friendships; there were misunderstandings and misinterpretations; and finally there were tendencies among the Romanticists with which Fichte heartily disagreed. Among the latter were indications that some of them inclined to aboslute monarchy and to Catholicism (Schelling and Friedrich Schlegel).[32] Fichte also believed that he saw leanings toward magic and alchemy, theosophy, and sexual irregularities, nor was he pleased by their romanticizing of the Middle Ages. All of these were virtually the opposite of his ideals, and he awaited an opportunity to attack these " aberrations."

The form of the attack was determined by several literary productions from the Romanticists. The first was an article by Novalis called *Die Christenheit oder Europa,* intended for publication in *Athena.* It never actually appeared in the journal because the friends of Novalis urged him not to publish it. The article was a glorification of " the idyllic times in which Europe as a whole was uniting its different provinces and states under a common interest, a vast spiritual realm, Christianity," a Christianity that was Catholic. The author went on to glorify the Middle Age and absolute monarchy, while he denounced the Reformation and the Revolution. He saw as an ideal the realization of the " new Europe " of his new conception.

The second production was Schlegel's lectures *Vorlesungen über die schöne Literatur und Kunst.* These lectures extended over the years from 1801 to 1804. The series of 1801-1802 was entitled *Die Kunstlehre,* that of 1801-1803 *Geschichte der klassischen Literatur,* that of 1803-1804 *Geschichte der romantischen Literatur.* The series of 1801-1803 was prefaced by a section entitled *All-*

---

[32] Haym, *op. cit.,* p. 924 *et seq.*

gemeine Übersicht des gegenwärtigen Zustandes der deutschen Literatur, and this suggested a title to Fichte.

The purpose of the essays comprising the *Grundzüge* is important for their understanding.   It explains their general content: the defense of a " reasonable religion " (not rationalism) against " Schwärmerei," the presentation of a series of historic periods, the defense of the Reformation and of the Revolution in so far as these events revealed freedom as the essence of the state, the reinterpretation of the term " Europe."   They are, in their purpose, a restatement of Fichte's belief in Reason, Freedom, Virtue, Protestantism, and the Rights of Man.

Die Grundzüge des gegenwärtigen Zeitalters propound Fichte's idea of the development of mankind.   History is divided into five great epochs:

1. the epoch in which Reason is governed completely by instinct: *the era of man's innocence.*

2. The epoch in which external compulsive authority is substituted for instinct: the age of positive systems of doctrine and life, which never go back to first principles and can therefore not convince, but merely wish to coerce, and demand blind faith and absolute obedience: *the era of original sin.*

3. The epoch of emancipation both from dominating authority and from the rule of instinct and Reason in every form: the age of complete indifference toward all truth and utter irresponsibility without any guide: *the era of complete sinfulness.*

4. The epoch of the science of Reason: the age in which truth is recognized as the highest good and is loved most: *the era of original justification.*

5. The epoch of the art of Reason: the age in which mankind with sure and unerring hand shapes itself to the

image of Reason: *the era of complete justification and sanctification.*

Fichte believed that his own age belonged to the third epoch.[33]

With this developmental idea in mind, Fichte proceeds to point out certain fundamental principles of human life. Some of these he has propounded before. Others represent novelties in his thought. Still others are in flat contradiction to some of his previous declarations.

The first of these principles is that man must not and cannot be considered as an individual, but always as part of society, that he is a unit within a whole. Fichte says:

It is the greatest error and the real basis for all other errors which are befuddling this age, when an individual imagines that he can exist, live, think and act for himself, and when he believes that he himself, his own person, is the object of his thought, since he is but a single unit in the general and necessary thought.[34]

This idea is repeated several times:

Looking at the thing as it is in truth we find that the individual does not exist; that he cannot count for anything, but must disappear completely; and that the group alone (*Gattung*) exists and it alone must be considered as existent.[35]

It is fortified and developed by the addition of ethical and religious arguments.

Reasonable life consists in this that the individual forgets himself in the group (*Gattung*), ties his life to the life of all and sacrifices himself for the whole; unreasonable life is this that the individual thinks of nothing but himself, loves nothing but himself and in relation to himself, and seeks nothing but his own

[33] *Werke*, vol. vii, pp. 11, 12, 18.
[34] *Werke*, vol. vii, pp. 23, 24.
[35] *Werke*, vol. vii, pp. 37, 38.

well-being.   And if that which is reasonable is at the same time
good and that which is unreasonable is evil, then there is but
one virtue: to forget oneself as an individual; and only one vice:
to think of oneself.[36]

Nothing individual can live in itself and for itself, but everything lives in the whole, and this whole in unbounded love constantly dies for itself, in order to live anew.[37]

Another fundamental principle of the *Grundzüge* is opposition to rationalism.   The idea that everything must be
understood and defined intellectually is rejected.   There are
other and more important elements in life, notably the
religious, which must receive their due.   Rationalism has
shown its evil results in its blind hatred of everything old
and established and in its attempts to substitute state constitutions built on vain and empty abstractions and on sounding
phrases, not realizing that firm and ruthless power is necessary to control and govern undisciplined generations.[38]

Indeed, it is time to understand the rôle of the hero, rather
than that of rationalism in human development.   Almost all
progress is attributable to the hero.   If we go back into the
history of the race we discover everywhere the hero at work.

Who has united the rude tribes and subjected the resisters to the
yoke of the laws and to peaceful life?   Who has kept them in
that state and preserved the existing states against dissolution
through inner disorder and against destruction by foreign
powers?   Whatever their names, they were all heroes, far in
advance of their age, giants in their surroundings both in physical and in intellectual power.   They subjugated generations to
their ideas of what ought to be and were roundly hated and
feared for that; sleepless they pondered through the nights,
concerned for those generations; without rest they marched from

[36] *Werke*, vol. vii, p. 35.
[37] *Werke*, vol. vii, p. 63.
[38] *Werke*, vol. vii, p. 30.

battlefield to battlefield, denying themselves all pleasures, often shedding their own blood.[39]

While their age round about them carelessly enjoyed its day, the heroes were lost in lonely thought, in order to discover a law, a causal nexus, which had aroused their astonishment, and whose discovery they most yearned for. They sacrificed pleasures and fortune, they neglected their own affairs, they wasted the finest flowers of their existence, and were ridiculed by the people as fools and dreamers. But their discoveries have been of great value to human life.[45]

The great and misunderstood heroes have had as their foil a thoughtless and rather stupid people. This is a striking idea. It does not appear very often, nor is it prominent in the treatise as a whole, but it is there [41] and points the way to a strange development in Fichte's thought.

Another development may be seen in the strong religious and ethical cast of thought carried into the field of politics. Words like " Religion," " Christianity," " love," " reverence " (*Ehrfurcht*), are repeatedly employed in the discussion. The sixteenth and seventeenth lectures are wholly religious. In the historical sections, moreover, Christianity is given a decisive place among the conditioning factors of the state. This growing mysticism or romanticism is highly significant. Details of its rôle in Fichte's thought will appear shortly.

The *Grundzüge* also contain a lengthy discussion of the state. The state, Fichte declares, is not a purely juridical institution.

The idea of the state most widely spread among German philosophers, that it is a purely juridical institution, is not unknown to us. We are opposing it with conscious deliberation.[42]

[39] *Werke*, vol. vii, pp. 46, 47.
[40] *Werke*, vol. vii, p. 52.
[41] See e. g. *Werke*, vol. vii, p. 89.
[42] *Werke*, vol. vii, p. 143.

Nor is the state purely an economic institution.[43]   The state has a threefold purpose:

1. it furthers culture and fights barbarism;
2. it brings nature under subjection;
3. it furthers the fine arts.[44]

As to the first point, the state has come into being largely for this purpose.   And this continues to be one of its primary purposes.   The second point involves the entire economic life.   It is the business of the state " to encourage industry, improve agriculture, perfect manufactures, factories, and machinery, to encourage inventions and discoveries in the mechanical arts and in the natural sciences." [45] Fine arts, finally, are essentially an off-shoot of the mechanical arts, and to them should be devoted the surplus energies of a people.

All the activities of the state are aimed, furthermore, at the establishment of freedom.   This is often a slow process, for freedom does not exist in the state of nature.   The state achieves freedom through law.   Great emphasis is placed on this idea.   It endows the laws of the state with an entirely new purpose.

Certainly we desire freedom, and should desire it, but true freedom emerges only by passing through the highest lawfulness.[46]

Finally the state is absolute in power.   It must have the means of enforcing its purpose.   It is definitely *Zwangsstaat*.   True wisdom requires that one understand this fact and that one merges one's individuality entirely in the state

[43] *Werke*, vol. vii, p. 157.
[44] *Werke*, vol. vii, pp. 162-165.
[45] *Werke*, vol. vii, p. 164.
[46] *Werke*, vol. vii, p. 210.

—willingly, it is to be hoped, but through compulsion if necessary.[47]

Nevertheless certain spheres are removed from the authority of the state, above all religion, philosophy (*Wissenschaft*), and virtue. These may be encouraged and furthered by the state, but the state does so indirectly and uses no compulsion in respect of them.[48]

Sharply differentiated from the state is the government. The form of the state is determined by eternal dictates of Reason, but the form of government is a matter for each age to determine for itself. How shall the form of government be determined? How shall those be chosen who wield the great power of government? There are two possible ways: either a general assembly of the people will elect the governors, or the people will entrust government to a special committee or to an individual. Details of the operation of government are not given.[49]

A notable contrast is made in these lectures between the Asiatic and the European state.[50] The Asiatic state has been a despotism. It originated through the subjugation of entire peoples by a despotic foreign group. The European state originated in another way. A small group of superior people settled among the barbarians. Through gifts and through definite benefits in the teaching of agriculture the newcomers attached the others to themselves. Because the newcomers were in a minority they had to respect the rights of their people and thus there arose in Europe a free people governed as equals under law. To this order of things Christianity was added. It found a group of small states whose people were free and equal. Its contribution to the

[47] *Werke*, vol. vii, p. 144.
[48] *Werke*, vol. vii, p. 166 *et seq.*
[49] *Werke*, vol. vii, pp. 154, 155, 159, 160.
[50] *Werke*, vol. vii, p. 174 *et seq.*

system was its recognition of the right of existence and sovereignty of the small state. At the same time it declared that before God all men were equal. Out of this religious freedom has arisen all personal freedom. And thus Christianity has given religious sanction to the sovereignty of states and to personal freedom.[51]

This leads Fichte to a peculiar use of the word " Europe." " Europe " is not a mere geographic expression. It is a religious and cultural unity. It is the basis for a cultural internationalism. Fichte does not wish to wipe out the small states. He points out that there has been a constant tendency to universal monarchy, because there has been a cultural unity in Europe. At the same time there are ways and means by which the individual state may survive. Similarly he denounces economic imperialism as an act committed against " Europe " as a whole.[52] Christianized " Europe," a cultural unity, is the real fatherland of every cultured person.

Since Christian Europeans are essentially one people, Europe in general must be considered as the one true fatherland and from one end to the other of Europe men must seek and be attracted by about the same things. They seek personal liberty, justice, and law equitable to all, which protects all without exception and delay, they seek opportunity to gain their livelihood through diligence and labor, they seek religious freedom for their confessions, they seek freedom to think according to their religious and philosophic principles and to express these freely and judge according to them. Where these things are denied them they long to emigrate; where they are granted they seek eagerly to immigrate.[53]

But it should be remembered that the individual states do

---

[51] *Werke*, vol. vii, p. 195 *et seq.*

[52] *Werke*, vol. vii, pp. 205, 206.

[53] *Werke*, vol. vii, p. 204 *et seq.*

not cease to be. They continue to exist and they strengthen themselves constantly in their individual existence. In this connection the oft-cited passage is found:

I ask you: Which is the fatherland of the truly educated, Christian European? In general, it is Europe, and especially in every age it is that state in Europe which stands at the height of culture. . . . May the earth-born who cling to the clod of ground, the river, the mountain, as their fatherland, remain citizens of the fallen state. They retain what they want and what makes them happy. But the sun-like spirit will be irresistibly drawn and turn wherever there is light and right. In this sense of world citizenship we may remain perfectly calm about the actions and the fate of the various states, as far as we and our children are concerned, to the end of time.[54]

We see here the continuance of Fichte's strong emphasis on social life against individualism; there is also the predominance of the state as juridic and economic institution, to which very definitely cultural functions are now added; there are also adumbrations, *obiter dicta,* of the contract theory; and the great emphasis on freedom remains. In contrast to his former adulation of the people we find him now severely critical of the people; and his own age is given a not too flattering place in the great scheme of world evolution; a theory of the " great man," the " hero," emerges but is only slightly developed. Finally, rationalism is definitely soft-pedaled and a strong religious note dominates the general tone.

Ideen über die innere Organisation der Universität Erlangen. 1805-1806

There was much discussion at this time about the reorganization of the Prussian universities. The German university of the eighteenth century was usually to be found

[54] *Werke*, vol. vii, p. 212.

in a small town and there it developed the type of "Gelehrte" who became the object of ridicule and satire. Carlyle's *Teufelsdroekh* at the University of *Weissnichtwo* is a caricature of a common type of German professor of the eighteenth century, a man far removed from the realities of life and far above any practical, not to speak of political, action. Fichte was by his very nature and by his philosophy of action opposed to a system which produced men of such type. His " Gelehrte " were to be men of the world, active in the service of the state and humanity. When therefore plans were being discussed as to the remaking of the university of Erlangen (then Prussian), he produced a memoir embodying his ideas on the subject.

Leaving aside other matters, there is one idea of importance for us in this memoir. Fichte insisted that the university should be controlled by the state and that its primary purpose was to render service to the state. He emphasized this idea against any educational provincialism, and also as a means of furthering common interests throughout Europe.

In order to break down provincialism Erlangen should invite students from all parts of Germany. And these young men, living together, would soon realize that they were all Germans. Thus a national German character would evolve over against the narrow provincialism then current. More than that, cosmopolitanism would inevitably develop. In a memorable passage he declared:

In this vigorous living together of youth from all the various states of the German fatherland, . . . something common remains in which all agree, namely German custom and German national character in general, and this is loved and honored by all. The special character of a people is therefore not lost; it is merely separated and understood in its emergence from the general national character. If furthermore, through an intelligent view of history, this latter is understood as arising out of

the general new-European character, then in place of the dull
and helpless patriotism (Spartanism, one might call it) a new
and really comprehensible patriotism arises which readily
reconciles cosmopolitanism and German national spirit, and in
every vigorous person this necessarily happens. This might be
termed Atticism. And thus is developed a servant of the state
capable and at home in all things.[55]

The memoir is important for us for two reasons: its allo-
cation of higher education to the state; and the development
of national character through education. It is also significant that national character and patriotism are easily recon-
cilable with cosmopolitanism.

Reden an die deutschen Krieger zu Anfange des Feldzuges 1806

This short fragment is a sketch of an address which
Fichte proposed to deliver to the German soldiers. He declares that he is a representative of philosophy and not
unknown. It is his duty to speak because the progress of
mankind is entrusted to his group. He had offered himself
as a fighter, but because of the faulty education of the
Germans the vocation of the warrior has been separated
from that of the scholar. Hence he has not been accepted
for active service. But talk he will.

Now that he can only talk, he wishes to speak swords and light-
ning, and that without consideration of danger and security.
He will speak the truth with clarity as he understands it, with
all the emphasis he is capable of, adding his signature to his
expressions, even though his utterances will certainly be worthy
of the death penalty before the courts of the enemy. But he
will not for that reason take refuge in cowardice, but he gives
you his word that he will either live in freedom with the fatherland or die with it as it perishes.[56]

[55] *Nachgelassene Werke*, vol. iii, p. 284.
[56] *Werke*, vol. vii, p. 510.

It is the soldier's duty to sacrifice his all. But this he would do for higher reasons: because of a true understanding of the meaning of life and because of a real sense of honor. This must be the ideal of the warrior:

Before the battle and in regard to the war: never to waver and to will nothing but the war, but at the same time to consider its ends with calmness and determination. *In* the battle: to maintain courage in the conflict and to think *eternal* thoughts, victory and the fatherland even in death. This opportunity belongs to you more than to others; for that reason you are to be envied. Through your example you will be a mighty influence on others and will arouse courage and strength in other parts of the nation which are now dead and exhausted. The friend of mankind and of the Germans looks up to you in hope. The hope of all the downcast is reposed in you.[57]

To this is added another short fragment entitled *In Beziehung auf den Namenlosen,* which is an attack on Napoleon as a usurper, for he has no idea of the purpose of the state and its basis in the will of the people.[58]

[57] *Werke*, vol. vii, p. 513.
[58] *Werke*, vol. vii, pp. 512-516.

CHAPTER V

Triumphant Nationalism

1806-1808

Der Patriotismus und Sein Gegenteil. Patriotische Dialoge. 1806 and 1807

In 1806 Napoleon invaded Prussia. At Jena and Auerstädt the Prussian parade troops succumbed to the French military machine. The Holy Roman Empire, venerable mummy these many years, was finally declared dead and placed in the museum of historical curiosities for future generations to contemplate. Fichte was greatly impressed by these events, as is disclosed by his later writings.

The first of these are the *Patriotic Dialogues,* two in number. They carry a double introduction, the first signed " Berlin – July, 1806," the second, " Königsberg — June, 1807." In other words these Dialogues bridged the tragedy of Prussia. The first was written in Berlin before the defeat at Jena; the second, after Fichte had fled to Königsberg following the disaster.

The *Dialogues* were occasioned by several articles which appeared in a magazine in which patriotism was extolled—patriotism being described as virtually identical with fawning flattery of the German princes.[1] This led to Fichte's answer in the form of a dialogue between A and B, in which B sets forth Fichte's views. They are bitterly satirical regarding narrow patriotism and at the same time amusingly egotistical as to their author's self-assumed importance in the philosophic thought of the time. It is in these *Dialogues*

[1] *Nachgelassene Werke*, vol. iii, p. 223.

that Fichte boldly declared that he alone of all men really understood Kant; more than that, he alone was capable of really clarifying Kant's ideas.[2]

The first *Dialogue* begins:

A.—(Embarassed and nervous, moves his chair about continuously and looks at the clock.)

B.—It seems as though my further presence is annoying to you. You wish to get rid of me. What's on your mind?

A.—If I must tell you frankly I should be very happy if you paid me a visit some other time. It is now five o'clock. This is the hour set aside in my daily schedule for the exercise of my patriotism. I neglect none of my duties more reluctantly than this.

B.—Well, are you in such a hurry? Exercise of patriotism? What do you do when you grow patriotic?

A.—I make inquiries as to what new public measures have been taken and what orders have been given; then I examine these for their wisdom and praise them loudly in public for their excellence.

B.—And do you always find these measures wise and praiseworthy?

A.—Of course. A good patriot must always praise everything about him and do nothing but praise. And should there really—contrary to all expectations—be something which cannot be praised, then he must pass this by in silence. In that way the beautiful tie of love and trust is established between the government and the governed. . . .[3]

After this introduction the dialogue drifts into a definition of the terms " patriotism " and " cosmopolitanism." [4]

B.—Cosmopolitanism is the will that the purpose of life and of man be attained in all mankind. Patriotism is the will that

[2] *Nachg. Werke*, vol. iii, p. 251.

[3] *Nachg. Werke*, vol. iii, p. 226.

[4] *Ibid.*, p. 228 *et seq.*

this purpose be attained first of all in that nation of which we are members, and the wish that this light may radiate from this nation over all mankind.

A.—Well, I'll accept that.

B.—Now if you will examine this definition a bit more closely you will discover that such a thing as cosmopolitanism is really impossible, but that in reality cosmopolitanism must necessarily become patriotism.

A.—I'm not afraid of looking at things more closely. Nevertheless your statement is so much in accord with my ideas that I shall permit you to examine the concept a bit closer.

B.—Every dominant will . . . can only become active in its surroundings. . . . Thus every cosmopolite necessarily, through his limitation by a nation, becomes a patriot. And every one who in his own nation is a strong and active patriot is thereby also a most active world citizen, because the final end of all national culture is always this, that it spread itself over all of mankind.

This is not very clear to A. So B. explains and finally puts the question:

B.—You are a German, are you not?

A.—No. I'm not a German. I do not want to be a German. I am a Prussian.[5] More than that, I am a patriotic Prussian.

B.—Understand me rightly. The separation of Prussians from the rest of the Germans is purely artificial. . . . The separation of the Germans from the other European nations is based on Nature. Through a common language and through common national characteristics which unite the Germans, they are separated from the others. . . .

A.—A common language for the Germans? That's true. But a common national character? Have the Germans a national character?

[5] I. H. Fichte edited away two attacks on Prussian particularism, by canceling the word " Prussian " before patriotism twice. Erben, *op. cit.*, p. 304.

B. affirms this and insists that the specific duty of the Prussian is to develop German national character. There are no specific Prussian duties except to labor for a unified monarchy which shall take its place in the system of European states. " That dark and confused idea of a separate patriotism is an offspring of lies and clumsy flattery." Then he continues :

B.—Let us summarize. The patriot wishes that the purpose of mankind be reached first of all in that nation of which he is a member. In our day this purpose can only be furthered by philosophy (*Wissenschaft*). Therefore philosophy and its widest possible dissemination in our day must be the immediate purpose of mankind, and no other purpose can or should be fixed for it.

The German patriot wishes that this purpose be attained first of all among the Germans and that from them it spread to the rest of mankind. The German can desire this, for in his midst philosophy has had its origin and it is developed in his language. It may be assumed that in that nation which has had the wisdom to conceive philosophy there should also rest the ability to understand it. Only the German can desire this, for only he, through the possession of philosophy and the possibility given thereby to understand it, can comprehend that this is the immediate purpose of mankind. This purpose is the only possible patriotic goal. Only the German can therefore be a patriot. Only he can, in the interest of his nation, include all mankind. Since the instinct of Reason has become extinct and the era of Egotism has begun, every other nation's patriotism is selfish, narrow, hostile to the rest of mankind.

B continues to instruct A in the fundamentals of true philosophy, that the state is not a mechanism which runs by experience or routine or by an act of God. The state is a product of Reason, and government is an art derived from Reason. He demonstrates that Prussian separatism is narrow and stupid and even un-German. There is also no need to decry every critic as unpatriotic, for the greatest patriot is often the severest critic. A's reply is that the people are, 99 out of a 100, ignoramuses and idiots, and all this is beyond them. Furthermore it is not patriotism. However, B expresses his belief that the people may be educated to understand it. Finally he declares that if the Germans do not take over the " government of the world through philosophy " the present cultural state will utterly disappear.

Thus the first Dialogue, written in times of peace before Jena. The second followed almost a year later, after the Prussian humiliation. What change did Napoleon's victory work in Fichte's ideas? This second Dialogue ought to contain first hand evidence as to that. It does. It begins:

A.—(answering B of the first Dialogue). That is the way you thought about patriotism a year ago, in the days of quiet, peace and security. Today I hope you have changed your mind since your actions seem to indicate that you have.

B.—Not in the least. It may be that my ideas have found application in another way, but they have not changed.

He goes on to re-affirm his former position. True, he is much devoted to Prussia at this time, but that is only due to the exigencies of the time, since the other Germans seem to have forgotten that they are Germans. There is a difference in the duties of a German in time of peace and in time of war. Now is the time for sacrifice and ceaseless labor to save Germany. But the important thing is to understand and live by true philosophy and Reason in the state. This understanding may come to the people through a great system of national education based on Pestalozzi's ideas. He concludes with the reflection that the annihilation of the Prussian army at Jena was due to the lack of a national

education.   Had a national education existed, every soldier
of the regular army might have deserted and yet a nation in
arms would have been ready to take up the fight and no
human power could have defeated them.

In these Dialogues there is again much that is old and
some that is new.   The discussion of the relationship
between patriotism and cosmopolitanism does not differ
radically from the similar ideas found in his lectures to the
Freemasons in 1800.   Furthermore the entire philosophic
basis of the state of Reason remains the same.   There also
appear short indications of the " hero " philosophy [6] and its
foil of an ignorant and helpless people.   New elements may
be found in his insistence on the cultural unity of Germany
with the need for political unity; the existence of a German
national character based on a common language and customs;
the need of a new national education following Pestalozzi;
and the mention, later fully developed, of " the people, the
nation, in arms."

*Episode über unser Zeitalter, aus einem republikanischen
Schriftsteller.*   1806-1807

This is the first of the Political Fragments written in
Königsberg after the defeat of Prussia at Jena.[7]   It is an
analysis of the causes of defeat.   Fichte declares that the
foremost phenomenon of the age is its arrested development.
Youth had made a magnificent start, only to fall back into
lazy complacency and stupidity in maturity.   This phenomenon might be witnessed among all classes.

Among literary men the first youthful productions were
the best.   When they had attained recognition they were
content to rest on their laurels.

In the army only the lower officers had any initiative,

[6] *Nachgel. Werke*, vol. iii, p. 235.
[7] *Werke*, vol. vii, pp. 519-529.

bravery, and alertness. The older and higher officers were lazy and careless, knew nothing of the enemy, and when the inevitable defeat came they were satisfied to conclude disgraceful treaties with the foreigner.

The upper classes were essentially selfish and sought only their own pleasures. They perceived the poverty and misery of the common people, but instead of bending all efforts toward alleviation and reform, their religion consisted of enjoyment of life. Only a few of them were vicious or malicious, the majority were merely " stupid and ignorant, cowardly, lazy, and degraded." Meanwhile the common people were reared in an other-worldly religion in order to divert their thoughts from the intolerable conditions of their present life.

The princes and rulers of the day were mainly engaged in conquering their neighbors or sitting idly by while their territories were despoiled. This " idiotic and inhuman " condition could be explained only by the education of the princes. They had been taught to be gracious to ladies, to talk French, to ride, to present arms, and to appreciate a little music and painting. The serious side of their education had been wholly neglected. No one had indicated to them what a state was and what their duties were within the state. " Whoever had dared to make this suggestion to them would soon have found his home in a madhouse." The flatterers and courtiers who surrounded them permitted them to become " indelible marks of shame " to their country and assured them that they were real fathers of the fatherland. The princes never heard a word of criticism, though their administration was nothing but an unbroken succession of errors.

The same was true of the ministers of state. They had little education to fit them for their positions. " In running through lecture rooms, if really they ever got that near, in assemblies, in coffee houses and gaming places, and perhaps in their travels " they had been prepared for their important offices. In foreign affairs they followed what they called " diplomacy " as their guiding star, that is, they wormed out state secrets and anecdotes and utilized them only for the purpose of insisting on procrastination in all important decisions. Their domestic policy might be summarized in their desire to accumulate a huge hoard of gold and silver. " They had not the least conception of the fact that the education of the people in religion and morality was the basis of all government." The moneys which they hoarded were used largely for the creation of an enormous army, well provided for in times of peace, well paid, well clothed, well armed. But in the first actual battle it collapsed utterly, so that a new army had to be formed. This was symptomatic of greater evils.

The nobility was likewise thoroughly useless for any serious work in the state. It held the high places in the army, but distinguished itself chiefly by " arrogant and rude interference and contemptuous defiance of all other classes." In battle some of them deserted the flag, others surrendered without offering resistance, still others enlisted their own people for service with the enemy. And yet they were mostly wealthy landowners, unmerciful to their own people, but very considerate to an invading army.

And to cap it all Germany was divided into two great powerful camps. Had they agreed, Germany would have had at least two units. But they were hostile and the smaller German princes allied themselves with one or the other. This virtually made for civil war and the utter helplessness of the country against any foreigner. These German princes

crawled before the foreigner; they opened to him the fatherland; they would have crawled before the Dey of Algiers and kissed the dust of his feet, given their daughters in marriage to his natural or adopted sons, if only thereby they might acquire the office they desired or might assume the title of king. Filled by their wild rapacity they never considered that the foreigner himself would despise them. . . .

This analysis speaks for itself. Its denunciation of the rulers as incapable and stupid and the cause of Germany's humiliation is balanced by the emphasis on faulty education.

Politische Fragmente: Die Republik der Deutschen zu Anfang des 22. Jahrhunderts. 1807

We get another glimpse of Fichte's thought at this time in the *Political Fragments* of 1807. One of these is called the *Republic of the Germans at the Beginning of the 22d Century.*[8] It was written after the defeat of Jena. Here is the opening:

The German nation had at a certain time become so degraded that some of its princes betrayed their country to the foreigner, and the rest who did not do this in quite the same way stood by as spectators in miserable cowardice and laziness and approved of it. The people, always under the simple, trustful illusion that it was their duty to suffer, since their princes desired it, were shamefully exploited, mocked and used as helpless pawns for every whim of the foreigner, even for the purpose of destroying Germans with Germans. The nobility proved itself the leading class of the nation only in this way that it was the first to flee when there was danger ahead, and by attempting to win the mercy of the common enemy through desertion of the common cause, through contemptible fawning and crawling, and through open treason.

As a result of this despicable attitude of the princes Germany disappeared from the map for a long time. After centuries it re-appeared, perhaps through the strength of the

[8] *Werke*, vol. vii, p. 530 *et seq.*

nation, perhaps through the work of a new generation of princes. The new Germany had a new constitution, built on the idea of infinite development through education. One of the ways in which this new education was to manifest itself was prophesied in this fragment.

The German republic found three Christian confessions. It added a fourth. This was called " General Christianity." It was intended for all free men. Since it embraced the fundamentals of all religion, most Germans joined this new " church," though worship in the older churches might continue for a time. But eventually the national church won over all others and then assumed the name of Christianity.

The confession of faith of this national church is very brief. The first article of the creed is the belief in freedom and independence. All belief in authority results from despotism and arises from the slave mind. The new Germans dare not have their freedom or intelligence limited by any authority.

The second and last article of the creed is an expressed belief in God and eternal life. The new church takes over the Bible as the " national book." The New Testament especially is found to be very valuable, while other portions can readily be interpreted for the purposes of the national church because of their vagueness. All religious instruction is based on the Bible.

The church itself is a beautiful building surrounded by a great open place. One of the first acts of the new church is to abolish burial and to substitute cremation. Special walls are erected which contain niches for burial urns. On the highest row are placed the urns of those who have died for the Fatherland on the field of honor. On the second row are those who have given counsel to the Fatherland with a clear mind. On the third row are those who as good fathers and mothers have lived in peace and brought brave children into the world and reared them for the Fatherland, and who have done good to their fellow citizens.

The church is surrounded by a beautiful garden, in which plants are gathered from all over the world. This collection of plants is sent to the people of the parish by such Germans of that parish as are residing in foreign parts, and serves as a symbol of their loyal and patriotic adherence to the Fatherland despite their absence from it. The preacher is a good botanist and cares for the plants with scientific solicitude. People from other parishes make pilgrimages to these botanical collections and compare them with their own.

The year starts with the Spring, an arrangement which agrees with Reason. Formerly another nation had adopted this custom, but " it was later found unworthy of this arrangement." Sunday remains as the day of church services.

On Sunday morning all the people of the parish gather before the church at an early hour. When all have arrived, the church doors are thrown open and amid soft music the congregation enters, each quietly taking his appointed place. The preacher is already at the altar. When all are seated the great curtains at the altar are drawn aside and the cannons, muskets, and other weapons which constitute the armory of the parish are revealed before the congregation.

For every German youth from his twentieth birthday to his death is a soldier. Then the justice of the peace appears before the congregation and unfurls the flag. This is the symbol of the civil congregation.

The first act of the service is the burial of the dead, or rather, the placing of the burial urns in their niches. The urns stand ready on the altar. If anyone has been buried by the older, sectarian churches, an empty urn is put on the altar for him. For this church embraces all. The burial proceeds according to the rank of precedence indicated above.

Then there is read in public the life story of the deceased which has been kept in detail in the records of the church.

The second great ceremony is that of receiving the new-born infants into the congregation. There are no privileges of sex. The boy or girl born first in that week is received first. The name of the child is entered on the records as the preacher lays his hand upon the child and says:

" We name you Maria Meyerin . . . (repeated by the congregation) as a sign that we, and through us the entire Fatherland of the German nation, recognize you as being *capable of Reason* (repeated by the congregation), *as one who is partaker in all rights of our citizenship* (repeated by the congregation), *as co-heir of eternal life, which also we hope for* (repeated by the congregation)."

When all have thus been received, the preacher blesses them with these words:

Live, grow and prosper! May the page in the record begun for you be the history of a moral life! May you join others in love which shall bind together all in the group in which you labor, and may brave sons and daughters take your place when you are taken from us! (Congregation joins in this.)

This astonishing fragment stands alone in Fichte's work. There is nothing in his previous thought to prepare us for it, and he recurred to it but once. The idea of a national church with purely nationalist ceremonies, national symbols (the flag and the collection of plants), and a national creed, intimately associated with universal military service, seems far removed from the universal note inherent in every consideration of the state thus far met with. Its points of resemblance to Jacobin nationalism in France are obvious. Fichte preached for Germany what French Jacobins practised.

Deducirter Plan einer zu Berlin zu errichtenden höheren Lehranstalt. 1807.

This is Fichte's idea of the nature and character of the new university to be founded in Berlin. Several supplements are attached to it.[9] It is not necessary to go into the general outline of his strictly educational plan. Several other matters, however, are of interest. It is worth noting that the university is sponsored by the state. Its purpose is to serve the state, the fatherland. This it does by developing teachers who will be active in the system of national education, by instructing its students in the nature of the state and teaching them to be capable servants of it, " for the fatherland has first claim on their services." [10]

Instruction is carried on in German, not in Latin, for real instruction can only be carried on in a living, a new, a creative language.[11] Students are not to be restricted to those from the " Prussian nation," but the attendance of students from all parts of Germany is to be proof of German brotherhood. In fact, the university is to be helpful in overcoming provincialism. Narrow clinging to the clod is not worthy of the man who is truly philosophical, of the free man whose vision transcends time and place. The fact that Bavarians and Prussians do not seem to recall their common Germanity is ridiculous and cannot be permitted at a university. No true statesman can develop from such narrow provincialism.[12] Finally it may be mentioned that the student pays his fees in grain money, which will eliminate all fluctuations in the value of fees.[13]

[9] *Werke*, vol. viii, pp. 97-204, 207-216, 216-219.
[10] *Werke*, vol. viii, p. 156.
[11] *Werke*, vol. viii, p. 165.
[12] *Werke*, vol. viii, pp. 168-171.
[13] *Werke*, vol. viii, pp. 166-167.

Über Machiavelli als Schriftsteller und Stellen aus seinen Schriften. 1807

The name of Machiavelli has been associated with everything devious in politics. It has been invoked to justify every form of deceit and even murder as a necessity of government. Webster's dictionary defines Machiavellianism as something " characterized by political cunning, duplicity, or bad faith." In the eighteenth century the name of Machiavelli was especially execrated. Frederick II of Prussia had spent part of his youthful energies writing his *Anti-Machiavell*, indicating that the Enlightened Monarchy of the age detested the Florentine's ideas.[14] The exception to this general attitude and perhaps the source of Fichte's ideas was the group of French Encyclopædists.

Fichte's short treatise on Machiaevelli was written in 1807.

Above all we find the noble Florentine misunderstood and measured by a standard which he particularly did not wish to have applied; he is furthermore maligned, execrated, his name used as a by-word; and finally his stupid and uncalled-for friends have dealt with him worse than his meanest detractors. We were just passing by and we came to love this person.[15]

After this introduction Fichte points out what attracts him to the ideas of the " noble Florentine." He does not go the full length of defending the intellectual and moral character of the author of *Il Principe*. He condemns his " morals," but attributes the fault to the age. Nevertheless he holds that *The Prince* is a valuable book of advice for all rulers. For its purpose was to " bring some order and sta-

---

[14] See Aldo Oberdorfer, " Machiavelli nel pensiero politico di J. G. Fichte," *Rivista d'Italia*, vol. 19 (2), 1916, pp. 285-332; also Couzinet, *Le Prince de Machiavelli et la théorie de l'absolutisme* (Paris, 1910).

[15] *Nachgelassene Werke*, vol. iii, p. 404.

bility into the incessant shiftiness of Italian political conditions." "No one can leave this magnificent spirit without love and respect, regretting at the same time that there was not vouchsafed to him a more pleasant theater for his observations."

Furthermore Fichte regrets the provincialism of Machiavelli. The Florentine was deeply devoted to his Florentine "republic" and opposed to all "monarchy." Only later, after his deposition and exile, did he rise to a larger vision, the contemplation of a united Italy, and then he extolled the unity of France and Spain.

In a section on Machiavelli's "paganism" Fichte defends his hero against attacks. "Christianity" in Machiavelli's day, he declares, was other-worldly in character and obscurantist in matters of culture. No wonder Machiavelli declared against it.

He also finds occasion to praise Machiavelli's age for its freedom of the press. The *History of Florence* was written at the instigation of Pope Clement VII. But when it was shown to contain a strong attack on the nepotism of this pope it was, together with other writings, forbidden by Clement. Yet the age read them. This holds true also of a comedy which contained the figure of a renegade monk and confessor. Other popes found no objection to these works; Leo even ordered the comedy produced in Rome. All this is a reproof for the censorship of Fichte's day. He also commends Machiavelli's *Seven Books on the Art of War*.

After this analysis of the important contributions of the Florentine, Fichte sums up his ideas in a section "In how far Machiavelli's politics still have application to our day." The basis of Machiavelli's political thought is contained in his maxim:

Everyone constituting a republic (or a state in general) and giving the laws to it must presuppose that all men are vicious (*bösartig*) and that without exception they will give expression to their viciousness as soon as they find a certain opportunity for it.

This is the basis of all politics and government. Without government there would be a war of all against all, the result of a general desire for exploitation. If this condition is to be removed there must be a strong government with compulsive powers, a *Zwangsstaat*. Even if Machiavelli's principle is not literally true, yet government must act as if it were. This rule may be applied both in domestic and in foreign policy, as long as chaos prevails. Now in domestic policy modern states, including Germany, have long since achieved a condition of order under law. Therefore in the administration of the state, in domestic policy, Machiavelli's maxim does not apply any more.

But in foreign relations it is different. There the war of all against all still exists. Inter-state relations are still in utter chaos. The strong overpower and exploit the weak at every opportunity. Not law and order, but self-preservation is still the supreme law. *Salus et decus populi suprema lex esto* in the relation to other states.

This fact needs emphasis. The eighteenth century had made current such ideas as " Humanity, Liberalism, and Popular Rights " (Humanität, Liberalität und Popularität), which led to a philosophy of the " golden mean, that is, the fusion of all contrasts to a dull chaos, hostility to all seriousness, all enthusiasm, all great ideas and resolutions." These ideas exercised an enervating influence at all courts and in all cabinets.

Since the French Revolution the doctrine of the Rights of Man and of Freedom and of the original Equality of all—which are certainly the eternal and indestructible bases of all social organization, against which no state dare offend, but with which alone no state can be erected or administered—have been accentuated too much by some of our own philosophers in the heat of battle . . . and this exaggeration has led to some disturbing results. . . . May it be permitted, then, that one who is not unknown and not without notoriety may rise from the dead and rectify these errors.[16]

There are those who have found in this treatise something foreign to Fichte's thought and who therefore find difficulty in interpreting it or even omit mention of it.[17]   On the whole, however, it seems to fit very well both into Fichte's system and into the times when it was written.   Especially the latter, for its preoccupation with the disturbed state of the country, with the need for German unity, with militarism, with weak and spineless government, with an inactive religion and with the freedom of the press, find ready parallels in Fichte's other writings of that period.   Furthermore, the idea of the compulsive state (*Zwangsstaat*) and the insistence on the Rights of Man as the basis of government occur in Fichte's thought years previously.

The new element is the insistence on a strong foreign policy.   This was born out of the situation then facing Germany, and especially Prussia.   Germany was divided at the time.   Some of its princes were allies of Napoleon and made it possible for him to fight Germans with Germans—a fact which Fichte already deplored on a previous occasion in the fragment *Die Republik der Deutschen*.   Thus this essay on Machiavelli is essentially a plea for a strong foreign policy in order that the state may be preserved.[18]

[16] *Nachgelassene Werke*, vol. iii, p. 428.

[17] E. g. Kuno Fischer.

[18] An interesting comparison is found in an unsigned article entitled " Fichtes Lehre von der äusseren Politik," in the *Süddeutsche Monats-*

Reden an die Deutsche Nation. 1807-1808

The famous *Addresses to the German Nation* were delivered in the Academy of Berlin in the winter of 1807-1808. They have had more than their share of attention both from patriotic Germans and from critical non-Germans. Fichte's son, in editing new editions in 1859 and 1870, called them " the political book of devotion of the Germans."

The *Reden* are the one work invariably associated with Fichte's name. On consulting the various histories of German literature, histories of the War of Liberation, histories of German culture, and the more general histories of Germany, it will be found that if and when Fichte's name is mentioned, it is in connection with the *Reden*. Max Adler was right: today, Fichte is highly praised by the Germans, but nobody reads him. Of all his works only the *Reden* are known, and for the most part they are misunderstood.[19]

It will be necessary therefore to devote some time to the *Reden,* in order that their real significance may be studied in detail. We shall have to examine their origin and their purpose, the sources drawn upon for their preparation, the conditions surrounding their delivery, their place in Fichte's thought, as well as their subsequent influence, and similar questions. Before doing this, it will be most convenient to outline their content briefly.

The *Addresses* begin with the statement that they are a continuation of the lectures of 1804, *Grundzüge des Gegenwärtigen Zeitalters.* In that series Fichte's era had been placed in the third great epoch of human development which he had called " the epoch of emancipation both from domin-

hefte, vol. xiv (1917), pp. 467-478. The anonymous author of South Germany was evidently attempting a criticism of the direction of foreign affairs in Berlin in 1917.

[19] Max Adler, *Wegweiser. Studien zur Geistesgeschichte des Sozialismus* (Stuttgart, 1914), chapter on Fichte, pp. 78-108.

ating authority and from the rule of instinct and Reason in every form: the age of complete indifference toward all truth and utter irresponsibility without any guide: *the era of complete sinfulness.*" In the three years that have since elapsed, this epoch, Fichte declares, has come to a complete close and a new epoch has begun. The *Addresses* are intended for Germans as such (*Deutsche schlechtweg*). Provincial particularism of any kind has no further right of existence.

Why did the former epoch pass? Why was it " the epoch of complete sinfulness?" Because it had been educated in a false philosophy; it was wholly individualistic and selfish. It had a wrong conception of society and the state. Ideals like Humanity, Liberalism, and Popular Rights (*Humanität, Liberalität und Popularität*) were dominant and these had really become synonymous with laziness and a behavior without dignity. Government was weak and ineffective and tried to insure its stability and continuation by leaning on foreign powers. A foolish " love of glory and national honor " had possessed the rulers. The nation was not living its own life, but was a part of a strange and foreign way of life. All this may be changed by a new education. This new education is not for any special group or class, but for the nation as a whole. For all development of mankind in Germany has always proceeded from the people. Nevertheless the educated classes have their part to play as leaders in this new education. "The dawn of a new world has already broken, the mountain tops are already gilded announcing the advent of the new day." (Lecture 1.)

What is the character of the new education by means of which the new day is to be ushered in? It is first of all an education of the will—" the real root of man himself." Hitherto education has proceeded on the theory that the student must retain free will. That is an error. The new education must produce a will that is moved by inner compulsion toward its goal.   More than that, it must develop an ardent love for the new life which it is endeavoring to create. But the new education is also concerned with a wholly new content.   It attempts to inculcate a new philosophy, which points out the eternal verities regarding man and his life in society.   Thus it becomes an education in Morals, yet even more than that, for essentially it becomes an education in Religion.   It will thereby become of great value to the state by producing men who are useful to society.   And it is the Germans above all who are capable of this new education. (Lect. 2, 3.)

But who are the Germans?   The nations of Europe (excluding the Slavs) are all of Germanic origin.   Yet there is a great difference between the Germanic peoples of Germany and those in other countries.   This is to be accounted for in two ways.   The Germanic tribes migrated into western Europe.   Some of them remained in what is at present Germany and fought off the influence of foreign races, cultures, and languages.   Others migrated to the present Latin countries, where they succumbed to foreign races, cultures, and language.   This fact is of the first importance, not, however, because they lived under a different climate (for climate makes very little difference), and not because they underwent a racial admixture with the Latin peoples, for in the Germanic homelands the admixture of Slavic blood was just as widespread.   No nation of Germanic origin can hope at the present time to prove its racial purity as against another.   The great difference lies in language.

Language is not something accidental or unimportant. Language is one of the most fundamental expressions of the soul of a people; it reveals its entire character.   A people (*Volk*) is a group that lives together, has the same language, and is subject to the same influence in its linguistic development. Now the distinctive characteristic of the Germans is the fact that they have an original language, while the other (Neo-Latin) peoples have an unoriginal, a borrowed, a mixed language. The Neo-Latin language characterizes the Neo-Latin peoples—both are unoriginal. The only comparison with the German language may be found in the Greek, which was also an original language.

The importance of this fact is especially attested by words that are applied to the super-sensuous, that transcend mere things, that designate ideas. Take, for example, those three famous [20] words *Humanity, Popularity,* and *Liberalism.* When these words came to the Germans, they misunderstood them, because they were foreign, and this helped to develop a lack of seriousness in the study of social conditions and other evils. Now had the German words been used— namely, *Menschenfreundlichkeit, Leutseligkeit,* and *Edelmuth*—the Germans would have understood at once and would not have been misled. The obvious inference is the desirability of using strictly German words, though Fichte himself sins very often against his own rule.[21] (Lect. 4).

---

[20] Fichte says " berüchtigt," which in modern usage is " infamous," " notorious," but the word has also the older meaning of " well-known," " famous," which seems better here, since he is not discarding the content of the words, but merely re-interpreting.

[21] Here are a few examples from the *Addresses* (they are by no means exhaustive) : Genie, genial, Nation, Natur, Unnatur, Historie, historisch, Monarchie, apriorisch, Germanier, germanisch, Idee, ideal, Idealisation, Klasse, Religion, Regent, Punkt, Interesse, Talent, Phantasie, Klima, Philosophie, philosophisch, Affekte, persönlich, Metakritik, Heros, Karikatur, humanistisch, Prosa, Barbarei, Romance, Triumph, Sylphe, klassisch, Tartarus, Titanen, Protestation, republikanisch, mechanisieren, Realität, Subjekt, Metaphysik, Spekulation, Ökonomie, heroisch, Charakter, etc. Already at the university, Fichte tried to improve his German by a method he apparently continued to practice : translation from other languages, especially French. See Johnsen, *op. cit.*, p. 10. Wechssler, " Die Auseinandersetzung des deutschen Geistes mit der franzö-

The importance of an original language such as German may be seen in a people's culture. The living language unites life with culture; the borrowed language divorces the two. The Germans, for example, have a real philosophy giving meaning and direction to life; another people will esteem " a very mediocre didactic poem on hypocrisy in comedy form as their greatest philosophic work."[22] Another illustration may be found in poetry. A living language produces a poetry that ennobles. The opposite will be found in the poetry known as " romance," whose themes are stale repetitions and whose language is stiff and formal, the whole detracting from the seriousness of life and cultivating mere playfulness. It is a shame for Germans to be attracted by such " foreign " trivialities. (Lect. 5.)

The influence of language may also be seen in history, above all in the Reformation. Christianity was something foreign to the Romans. It became the possession of the educated classes. It was left for "that German man Luther " to bring religion back to the people. And the German princes stood by him in this effort. German seriousness and depth stood against foreign frivolity and shallowness. Accordingly German philosophy also became religious, while in foreign countries philosophy was a synonym for irreligion and atheism. This is also reflected in education. Germans learned that it is the task of education to develop the entire man, to teach him his place and duties in the state, and finally to train the nation in its mission to humanity. And such education has been meant for all the people, not merely for a single class. The free German cities of the Middle Age already showed the vast difference

---

sischen Aufklärung (1732-1832)," *Deutsche Vierteljahr. f. Literaturwissensch. u. Geistesgesch.*, vol. i (1923), p. 631. Max Wundt, *Fichte Forschungen*, "Fichtes Sprache," pp. 373-374.

[22] Molière's *Tartuffe*.

between Germans and others. They prefigured the truth that "the German nation alone among the neo-European nations . . . can endure a republican constitution." The Germans ought therefore to produce "an inspiring history of the Germans of this period, which would be a national and popular book, such as the Bible and the hymnal." (Lect. 6.)

The nature of the state and of government can only be understood through true philosophy. The "foreign" idea of the state is that of a mechanism designed to compel obedience. The German conception is that of a system of education that both instructs the mind as to the real nature of the state and educates the will freely to accept its ordinances. Therein lies true freedom. And this German conception does not imply any narrowness or exclusiveness, but is animated by a universal and cosmopolitan spirit. (Lect. 7.)

The Germans as the *Urvolk*,[23] the original people, have learned to regard the state and the nation with truly religious spirit. Not in the manner of tyrants who preach religion as a cloak of despotism, urging submission, but in the manner of freemen who have learned to love their nation. For "a nation is the totality of all those living together in society, continuing its kind physically and spiritually, living under a special law of the development of the divine out of itself."[24] This law of development produces national character. Since the divine is active in the nation, the attitude of the German toward it is love. Love of the nation animates both the people and the government. Patriotism must rule the state,

[23] The word implies the idea of an "elect people." See Léon, *op. cit.,* vol. ii, p. 441, note.

[24] J. Holland Rose, *op. cit.,* also reproduces this definition (in another translation), but he significantly omits the word "spiritually," an important omission.

but it must be a patriotism based on love. Thus may freedom exist and thrive; thus also may the state set itself higher aims than the protection of its citizens and their property, peace, and well-being. Only such nations have survived as have loved freedom and hated slavery, as have been consumed by the divine flame of love for the fatherland, and as have been inspired by things eternal. The state must find its chief task in the education of its citizens for these higher ends. (Lect. 8.)

The new education is to be a complete re-creation of mankind, and the best system yet devised for it is that of Pestalozzi. Pestalozzi's system aims to educate the will to spiritual freedom. The new education cannot be left to parents and the home. These have failed signally in the past. There must be a complete separation of the children from the home. How much of national education may still be left to the home—if any—is still a matter for deliberation. But essentially education must be the business of the state. It must be based on the belief in freedom and in the infinite development and perfectibility of mankind, on the faith that Germans will become philosophers who understand the purpose and method of life. In regard to the state it will inculcate the idea that mutual respect demands of all that they submit themselves to the whole freely and gladly. Both sexes are to be educated without differentiation for both shall aim at perfect humanity. The schools shall be miniature states. The students learn the three R's. They are also instructed in the crafts. They learn about agriculture and cattle-raising. They are taught to operate machines. Every article of food and clothing is produced by the students. Their school community must be self-sufficient. This is the general education through which all must pass. Then there is the special education for scholars. Only the very best are chosen for this education. These are thoroughly trained in the arts and sciences, in the art of government, and in all higher learning. No distinction of class is made in the choice of these specialists. The selection is made solely on the basis of talent. This new education does not neglect the bodies of the students. A good physician should be asked to work out the best system of physical training which shall be generally applied. (Lectures 9, 10.)

All these things will contribute to the creation of the new nation which is to arise in Germany. If these ideas were followed, many other problems would find immediate solution. Take the army, for instance. Most of the revenues of the state now go toward the upkeep of a huge army. In the new nation this would be unnecessary, for there would be a people's army, a nation in arms, created by the new system of physical training.[25] If all would co-operate the new nation might already come into being in twenty-five years. But that is hardly to be expected. There will be opposition. Then the state ought to intervene and compel such recalcitrants to submit to the new education and thus to help create the new nation.

The creation of the new nation is necessary for the preservation of Germany. If Germany disappears politically her language will also disappear, likewise her literature. There is no hope of preserving a cultural Germany without a political Germany. For culture is built on the state. Therefore Germans should not grow despondent or cowardly, they should not adopt the spirit of slaves and become submissive. (Lect. 12.)

Under the circumstances what can the Germans do? In

[25] Nations arising from national humiliation have frequently paid much attention to physical training and athletics. Fichte's age witnessed the rise of the *Turner* under Jahn. The Czechs brought forth the *sokols*. Germany since the World War has witnessed an astonishing development of athleticism.

the first place they must see to their frontiers. The first frontiers are those of language and nature. Rivers and mountains are natural boundaries within which a people develops. The next step ought to be the closing of the state commercially. The German has all he needs within his boundaries, and nothing has been more harmful to him than the striving after universal monarchy. Nor does he have need to try to capture world commerce and establish an economic empire.

How does the freedom of the seas, or international trade, or the booty of other hemispheres concern the German? He does not need them. He has a richly endowed land and his industry affords him everything that a cultured man needs for life. . . . O if only a happy fate might have preserved the Germans as much from indirect participation in the booty of the other hemisphere as it did in the direct. . . . May we at last recognize that while the airy theories about international trade and manufacturing for the world may do for the foreigner, and belong to the weapons with which he has always invaded us, they have no application to Germans, and that, next to unity among ourselves, internal independence and commercial self-reliance are the second means to our salvation, and through them to the welfare of Europe." [26]

The conflict at arms is past; now comes the new conflict of principles, of customs, of character.   (Lecture 13.)

The last Address (14) is a grand peroration, a fervent appeal to all in Germany, young and old, man, woman and child, educated and uneducated, to give their active support to the gigantic task of creating the new German nation.

Such, in outline, are the famous *Addresses to the German Nation*. The first and most necessary comment is that they

[26] This powerful anti-imperialist blast has been used with great effect against modern Germany by W. H. Dawson, *The Evolution of Modern Germany* (London, 1908), p. 4.

contain hardly anything new. Practically every idea in them has appeared previously in Fichte. There is the Moral Universe, the emphasis on freedom, the importance of education, Pestalozzi, the nation in arms, the closed commercial state, the cultural mission of the state, the republican organization of the state, etc; coupled with a strong appeal against imperialism. Highly significant is the fact that Fichte reiterates the cosmopolitan goal of the new German nation. Its real purpose is to be the leader of mankind in its spiritual evolution.

There are new things in the *Addresses.* Minor matters, such as the new physical education, and the disdain for climate and race in the formation of national character, need not detain us. What is important is the emphasis on language, and the designation of the Germans as the *Urvolk,* the elect people. This leads us to a consideration of various questions, such as the origin and purpose of the *Reden,* their sources, the conditions surrounding their delivery, their influence, etc.

The Purpose of the Reden

On Nov. 28, 1807, the following notice appeared in the *Vossische Zeitung:*

I shall resume my lectures of the winter semester for the public of both sexes on Sunday at the customary hour from 12 to 1 and I shall carry down to the present the considerations which I began three years ago and which appeared under the title *Grundzüge des gegenwärtigen Zeitalters.* I shall announce in this journal the beginning of these lectures.

Berlin, Nov. 26, 1807. FICHTE

On December 10, 1807 the *Vossische Zeitung* carried the further notice:

My lectures which are a continuation of the *Grundzüge des*

gegenwärtigen Zeitalters will begin next Sunday, Dec. 13, from 12 to 1, in the amphitheater of the Academy.

FICHTE [27]

The same purpose is stated in the opening sentence of the *Reden.*

The *Grundzüge* of 1804 had been directed against the " aberrations " of the Romanticists. They opposed Catholicism and upheld Protestantism and the Reformation; against the idealized Middle Ages and the romantic literature of those centuries they upheld " religion " and " Christianity "; against the monarchic tendencies and the condemnation of the Revolution they stood for republicanism and " freedom "; against " mysticism " and " *Schwärmerei* " they propounded the rule of " Reason "; against " naturalism " they held up the ideal of a Moral Universe.

The actual content of the *Grundzüge,* though interpreted in a wholly different way, had been taken largely from Schlegel's lectures, *Vorlesungen über die schöne Literatur und Kunst.* With this in mind it is easy to trace the continuation of the series of 1804. Here again is the defence of the Reformation and the Revolution: the emphasis on " religion " and republicanism; the insistence on the Moral Universe and the rule of Reason and Philosophy; the scorn for medieval " romance "; the denunciation of the lazy and irresponsible princes; the idealization of the *Volk.*

Similarly the dependence on Schlegel for the actual content of the *Reden* is also evident. In Schlegel, Fichte found the source for his materials on language. It was Schlegel who made the distinction between the Germans who remained in Germany and those who migrated to other countries. It was Schlegel who declared language to be the key to national character. It was Schlegel who emphasized the difference

[27] Léon, *op. cit.,* p. 61, note 2.

between the neo-Latin (Schlegel's term: *neu-Lateinische*) languages and the German. It was Schlegel who idealized the early Germans.[28] The term *Urvolk* in the sense of an " elect people " was borrowed from Schelling and Novalis.

It might be mentioned also that during the writing of the *Reden* Fichte spent much time in reading Tacitus' *Germania*,[29] that idealized sermon on the early Germans preached to a " corrupt generation of Romans." This accounts for some of the more florid parts of the *Reden*. During the same period he was immersed in a re-reading of Pestalozzi. He wrote to his wife in 1807:

I am now studying the educational system of this man [Pestalozzi] and I find in it the real curative for sick mankind.[30]

Schlegel and the Romanticists, Tacitus and Pestalozzi are thus imbedded in Fichte's philosophy.

But if the link between the *Grundzüge* and the *Reden* is certain—and it is—there is a difference of circumstance. The time has changed from peace to war, from security to insecurity, from a distant aloofness from world affairs to the presence of an army of occupation in the Prussian capital. Fichte was always *zeitgemäss* in his popular lectures. It was inevitable that he should be so here. Nonetheless the *Reden* are not essentially " war-talks "—no doubt the French would not have permitted them as such. They are hardly even political speeches, but rather educational and pedagogic advice. If Napoleon [31] and the French are mentioned at all, it is always as cultural opponents.

[28] Schlegel's *Kunstlehre* is the source for most of these ideas. His *Geschichte der romantischen Literatur* contains others. For detailed references see Léon, *op. cit.*, vol. ii, pp. 422-433; vol. iii, pp. 67-68.

[29] *Fichtes Leben*, vol. i, p. 427.

[30] *Fichtes Leben*, vol. i, p. 389.

[31] Heinrich Scholz, " Fichte und Napoleon " in *Preussische Jahrbücher*, vol. 152 (1913), pp. 1-2, sees in the " Mahomet " of the Eighth Address a reference to Napoleon.

The Delivery of the Reden

The *Reden* were delivered on Sundays between the hours of 12 and 1 to audiences which were very meager. The announcement that they were a continuation of the lectures of 1804 put them out of the range of interest of most people. The price of admission was very high, it being fixed at one Reichstaler. They attracted hardly any notice in the press.[32]

There is a persistent note even in Fichte's day as to the great danger to which the author exposed himself in delivering the *Reden,* making it appear as an act of great personal heroism. Thus in the *Reden* Fichte himself stated:

My personal danger need not be considered. It could be used to great advantage. My family and my son would not lack the help of a nation given to the family of a martyr. This would be the best outcome. I could not use my life in a better way.[33]

Again he warns against the interpretation that he is arousing the people to arms against the invader:

These lectures are not intended to incite action that disturbs the peace. On the contrary I would warn earnestly against that as leading to disaster.[34]

In a letter to Beyme in January, 1808, Fichte wrote:

I know the risk. I know that a bullet may strike me down as well as Palm. But that is not what I fear, and for the aim I have in view I would gladly die.[35]

[32] For these and the following materials see the excellent article of Rud. Koerner, " Die Wirkungen der Reden Fichtes," in *Forschungen zur Brandenb.-Preuss. Geschichte,* vol. 40, part 1 (1927), pp. 65-87.

[33] *Werke*, vol. vii, p. 457.

[34] Twelfth Address.

[35] *Fichtes Leben.* Also cited in J. H. Rose, *Nationality in Modern History,* p. 49.

At the end of 1808 Fichte's wife wrote a letter to Charlotte Schiller (Dec. 20, 1808), in which she said:

The book [the *Reden*] has cost me much fear, the treatment of unfortunate Palm always rising before me. I could not sleep peacefully a single night, as long as the foreigners, who have frightened many people out of their wits, were here. The book is written with deepest love, the strongest sense of duty and loyalty. For the author knew full well that he was incurring danger and I thank God from the bottom of my heart that all storms have fortunately passed.[36]

Another item is worth citing in this connection, for it appears to be the source for the further elaboration of the " danger stories" connected with the *Reden*. In 1822 (Sept. 19) Ludwig Robert, a patriotic poet, published a newspaper article in which the following passage occurs:

Die Reden an die deutsche Nation [were directed against] the despotism of Napoleon, against his spirit of conquest, against his system of exploitation. [They aimed] to arouse the German people to a knowledge of its own importance, to raise its courage. They were delivered in Berlin in the Academy, while a French Marshall was governor of the city, while regiments with bands playing passed by, while spies were scattered in the audience, so that none of the latter, who were richly rewarded, had the courage to look up.[37]

The development is obvious. Suffice it here to underline the date—1822—that is, fifteen years *post eventum*.

This story is further developed by Fichte's son, I. H. Fichte, when he edited his father's Complete Works in 1845. He writes:

Thus he delivered the *Reden an die Deutschen* in the winter

[36] *Fichtes Leben*, vol. ii, p. 408.
[37] Cited in *Fichtes Leben*, vol. i, p. 425.

months of the years 1807-1808 in the Academy Building in Berlin, while his voice was often unheard because of the French drums passing through the streets, and while well-known spies were in the room. Several times the rumor was current in the city, that he had been seized by the enemy and carried off. He was never molested by the enemy, who seemed to take not the least notice of his undertaking, with the exception of a short notice in the *Moniteur,* that a famous German philosopher was delivering lectures in Berlin on the improvement of education; concerning the reasons for this forbearance or oversight we really have only vague surmises.

Even later, at the time of the evacuation of Berlin by the French, when one of the rudest minions, Davoust, in order to frighten and paralyze even from a distance, called together some of the prominent writers of Berlin such as Schmalz, Hanstein, Wolf, and Schleiermacher, and threatened them, amid execrations of their king and country, should they say or write anything about politics or the German situation: even then Fichte remained unnoticed, either by chance or on purpose.

Yet he was the only one who expressed himself openly and emphatically against the foreign domination. Meanwhile, during the time of delivery, he had already taken the precaution to have them appear simultaneously in print, so that the current rumors concerning his utterances might be immediately corrected or at least thoroughly refuted by authentic testimony.[38]

Several years later, according to the son, when Fichte resigned from the University of Berlin, his resignation was accepted with the comment, that " because of the *Reden an die deutsche Nation* he had a bad reputation with the French authorities." [39]

These stories of the danger that surrounded the delivery of the *Reden,* are repeated by most writers on Fichte. Nevertheless there are grave doubts as to the truth of the

[38] *Fichtes Leben,* vol. i, p. 422.
[39] *Fichtes Leben,* vol. i, p. 437.

tradition. The arguments against the story are found in
its very sources. True, Fichte no doubt thought there was
cause for fear. His wife substantiates the atmosphere of
fear in her letter to Charlotte Schiller, but this was written
a year after the beginning of the Addresses. When the story
appears again, we find it in a very much more elaborated
form with parading French troops, spies, etc. filling in the
picture. But this is fifteen years later and in an article by
a patriotic poet. Fichte's son takes over the same account
almost forty years after the events. But here, in part, we
find the criticism which threatens to relegate the entire story
to the realm of legend.

Why did the French pay no attention whatever to Fichte?
If a notice of the *Addresses* appeared in the *Moniteur* why
were the *Addresses* characterized there as " lectures on the
reform of education "? When Davoust in 1808 summoned
the literary men of Berlin, including many minor figures—
Iffland, Heinsius, Sack, Bucholz, August, Kuhn, Benecke,
Schmalz,—why was not the " only man who had dared to
express himself openly and emphatically against foreign
domination " omitted? [40] Is there not something strange in
the fact that the French left their greatest enemy thus free
to carry on? J. Holland Rose feels something of this dis-
crepancy when he writes:

Considering Napoleon's dread of the principle of nationality, it
is strange that he did not accord to Fichte the doom meted out
to Palm for a much slighter offence.[41]

The probable answer to the " strange " action of the
French is that they knew nothing of the *Reden* and that the
whole story of the danger incurred and the heroism shown
by Fichte is a fear complex brought on by the execution of

[40] See Koerner, *op. cit.*, for these names, p. 69.
[41] *Cambridge Modern History*, vol. ix, p. 326.

Palm, the Nürnberg book-seller, on August 25, 1807, for circulating a rather mild anti-French pamphlet entitled *Deutschland in seiner tiefen Erniedrigung*. This ruthless act created a panic in Germany, of which the recurrence of Palm's name in Fichte's correspondence is ample proof. Fichte himself and his wife were undoubtedly filled with fear and trembling. But there does not appear to have been the slightest danger for him, since his *Addresses* went unnoticed. The details of the story about the spies, etc. are evidently the creation of a later patriotic legend. This leads to a closely related problem.

The Influence of Fichte's Reden

It has generally been assumed that Fichte's *Reden* were of very great importance in the German Wars of Liberation. It is easy to understand the basis of such an assumption. Fichte had supposedly aroused a people utterly indifferent to the fate of their country to a high degree of patriotism and this had then asserted itself in the expulsion of the foreign enemy. In accordance with this idea, Fichte is given credit for having influenced the great men and movements of his time, the reforms of Stein, the founding of the university of Berlin, the general remaking of education, etc.[42]

In support of this thesis various data have been adduced. Thus, for instance, we may find in the Correspondence of Fichte several letters which are full of praise of the *Reden,* notably those of Wagner,[43] Fellenberg,[44] and Pestalozzi.[45] Fichte's wife also thanks Charlotte von Schiller for her

---

[42] Spranger, "Altensteins Denkschrift von 1807 und ihre Beziehungen zur Philosophie," in *Forschungen zur Brandenburgisch- und Preussischen Geschichte*, vol. xviii (1905), pp. 471-517, makes out a case for Fichte's influence on Hardenberg's Riga memorial of 1807.

[43] *Fichtes Leben*, vol. ii, p. 459.

[44] *Ibid.*, vol. ii, p. 561.

[45] *Ibid.*, vol. ii, p. 566.

words of praise.[46]   A letter of Beyme to Fichte in February,
1808, which was included in the first edition of *Fichtes Leben,*
but omitted in the second, speaks very highly of the *Reden*
and declares that Stein read them.[47]   Koerner further mentions Altenstein, Schlichtegroll, and Oerstedt as expressing
favorable opinions.   Wilhelm and Carolina Humboldt state
that the *Reden* were used " *wie ein Art Gebetbuch* " in the
Laroche family.[48]

But any great immediate influence of Fichte's *Reden* is
subject to serious doubts.   As early as 1862 Jürgen Bona
Meyer denied their effectiveness and declared that the contemporaries were silent concerning them.[49]   This criticism
was taken up and elaborated by Körner in the article already
mentioned in the *Forschungen zur Brandenburgisch und
Preussischen Geschichte* in 1927.   Körner's argument is
reproduced here.

That the *Reden* were delivered before a very small audience has been noted.   The notice in the *Moniteur* is apparently a legend.   Not a single Berlin paper noticed the *Reden.*
There was therefore no general enthusiasm over them.   The

[46] *Fichtes Leben,* vol. ii, p. 408.

[47] Hans Schulz, " Aus Fichtes Leben—Briefe und Mitteilungen zu einer
künftigen Sammlung von Fichtes Briefwechsel," *Kantstudien,* Ergän-
zungshefte No. 44 (1918), pp. 60-61.   Seeley's *Life and Times of Stein*
makes the same statement, but it is taken from Stein's autobiography
written in 1823-24.   In another passage Seeley declares that " Fichte's
lectures passed unnoticed " (part v, ch. iv).

[48] Koerner, *op. cit.,* p. 66 *et seq.*

[49] Friedrich Janson tried to refute Meyer and ascribed to the *Reden* a
very great influence.   But he offers little evidence in support of his contention.   See Fr. Janson, *Fichtes Reden an die deutsche Nation* (Berlin
und Leipzig, 1911), in *Abhandlungen zur Mittleren und Neueren Geschichte,* Heft 33.   Similarly Janson's related study, *Fichtes Reform-
pläne in den " Reden an die deutsche Nation " und ihr Zusammenhang
mit den praktischen Reformen nach 1806* (Berlin and Leipzig, 1911),
which emphasizes educational reform.

attention they received in the rest of Germany may be gauged by a note in the (Berlin) *Allgemeine Zeitung* (no. 47, 1808) on January 16, 1808 when five of the *Reden* had been delivered. The note read: "Königsberg, January 16. Fichte who came here from Berlin could not prosper here and returned to Berlin." Not a word about the *Reden*. When the *Reden* were printed, very few reviews appeared in any journals, and some of these were extremely unfavorable.[50]

Körner has combed the leading correspondence of the day in order to discover references to the *Reden*. He included men like Ernst Moritz Arndt, Jahn, Gneisenau, Scharnhorst, Schleiermacher, Niebuhr, Uhland, and Goethe and covered the period from 1807 to 1813. The *Reden* are not mentioned once in this correspondence.

He continued with the fifty outstanding autobiographies and diaries between 1808 and 1813, including the works of Arndt, Delbrück, Hufeland, Kohlrausch, and others. In all of them he was unable to discover a single reference to Fichte and his influence on their life or that of his day.

The ignoring of Fichte by Davoust in 1808 when he included many minor men in his warning has been mentioned. It is significant enough to repeat here.[51]

---

[50] Another recent Fichte student, Gertrud Bäumer, also recognizes the legend. She writes in *Fichte und sein Werk* (Berlin, 1921): "It is very doubtful whether he exerted a strong influence on his times, yes, whether he even belongs to the historically formative forces of his day. The *Reden an die deutsche Nation* were certainly intelligible in their ideas to only very few. The practical suggestions which he develops in them were more or less impracticable, that is, extravagant, unstatesmanlike. In the whole construction of the *Reden* there is much that is forced and artificial, much that is merely logical scheme, much that is doctrinaire" (p. 108). Janson points out another cause for their failure. Their language is "abstrakt, unpraktisch, beziehungslos." (*Fichtes Reden*, p. 7.)

[51] This argument *e silentio* may be supplemented by another observation. The letters of praise printed in *Fichtes Leben* and mentioned above

The argument from silence is always precarious. There is, however, more positive evidence. When Fichte endeavored to have the *Addresses* printed, they were at once held up by the Censorship of Prussia. Nolte wanted to refuse publication for the criticism of Prussia contained in the First Address. The chief objection against them was that they were too liberal. They spoke too much of freedom and republics. Each lecture had to pass the Censor individually. At one time the officials tried to suppress the Thirteenth Address by pretending that they had lost it. Finally they were passed with great reluctance.[52]

The book appeared in 1808 and was a publisher's failure. Fichte sent it to his father who did not even read it. No new edition of the *Reden* was attempted till 1822. When they were to be published in Prussia, the Censor promptly forbade the book, because it "nourished deceitful and empty phantoms." [53] The new edition had to be printed in Leipzig.

Instead of enthusiasm or even approval, the *Reden* met with much criticism. The idea that the age was corrupt was openly ridiculed. Many resented the criticism of the state and of religion. Fichte was not popular personally and many sneered at his egotism and the identification of his philosophy with "Deutschtum." Some were angered at his cosmopolitanism, others by his opposition to armed revolt,

are almost all from people who are asking a special favor from Fichte. Their praise is tacked to the request they have to make. As to Pestalozzi's letter, it is quite obvious that he did not read the *Addresses* with their rather strong criticism of his ideas. His letter speaks merely in general terms of the importance of education and is written one year after publication of the *Reden*.

[52] Max Lehmann, "Fichte's Reden an die deutsche Nation vor der preussischen Zensur," *Preussische Jahrbücher*, vol. 82 (1895), pp. 501-515.

[53] Introduction to the edition of 1870 by I. H. Fichte, p. xiv.

still others at his praise of Napoleon in the Twelfth Address. Kleist was furious over the reference to love of glory and national honor as deceitful phantoms.[54]   Mueller scorned an educational program which could be effective in twenty-five years.   Jean Paul declared that Fichte erred greatly " in supposing that much that was old, e. g. in education, love of country, was his original idea; he believes that he is blazing every trail over which he travels."   As late as 1818 Kotzebue sneered (in the *Literarisches Wochenblatt*): " Outside of Herr von Passow nobody seems to have noticed that the French feared Fichte."

In 1815-1816 there was an eager debate in the intellectual circles of Berlin, in which Niebuhr, Wieland, Schmalz, and others, participated, as to the cause of German revival.   Not once was Fichte's name mentioned in these discussions.

We see the same thing among the historians.   Many histories of the period were written by the Germans; that of Hormayr in 1819, that of Manso in 1820, that of Dresch in 1824, that of Rotteck in 1826, that of Hasse in 1816 and following, that of Wachler in 1835, that of Bassenitz in 1851.   Not one of these mentions Fichte.   Even Ranke's *Hardenberg* of 1877 has not a word about the *Addresses*.

All of this is significant.   It would seem to point to the conclusion that the usual conception about the addresses and their influence is wholly legendary.   Whatever influence the *Addresses* had belongs to a later period, a consideration of which will have to be left to another chapter.

The Interpretation of the Reden

The place of Fichte's *Reden* in the sum total of his thought will be discussed later.   A few general comments are in order, however.   There is no doubt that the defeat at Jena

[54] " Liebe zum Ruhm und Nationalehre sind täuschende Trugbilder." First Address.

stirred Fichte deeply. This was reflected in many of his letters. In one of them [55] he wrote from Königsberg:

At the end of last year in a letter to the king I declared that only my devotion to his just cause persuaded me to leave the provinces occupied by the enemy and to come here. This devotion shall continue to be sacred with me, even in case the king should have no country at all. Even in a foreign country I shall consider myself as one who is in his service, keep myself ready to hurry on at the slightest suggestion, and should an opportunity present itself I shall enter into no permanent engagements in a foreign country without his express permission.

This is proof sufficient that Fichte was filled with patriotism and love of country at this time. There are other evidences. The *Reden* themselves breathe a different spirit from all his other work. Formerly he discussed the state virtually in the abstract, at least with much detachment. In the *Reden* there is a real enthusiasm for Germany. It is carried to extremes. Germany is identified with everything good, foreign countries and cultures with everything evil. In Walz' happy phrase Fichte had heretofore theorized about the state; here was a definite and enthusiastic " experience of the state." [56] Thus far, then, the *Reden* are patriotic and nationalistic.

But a word of caution is necessary. Fichte's patriotism of these years was far more an opposition to the foreign invader than approval of the Prussian state or German conditions. The psychology of this is readily understood. An army of occupation invariably tends to create a strong nationalism in the occupied country; even a mild internationalism has a difficult time to survive, since it is almost synonymous with betrayal of the homeland. In other words, an

[55] To Altenstein, June 2, 1807. Hans Schulz, *Aus Fichtes Leben*, p. 53.

[56] G. A. Walz, *Die Staatsidee des Rationalismus und der Romantik und die Staatsphilosophie Fichtes* (Berlin, 1928), p. 589: " nicht mehr Staatstheorien, sondern Staatserleben."

army of occupation creates a war psychology: the opposition
to the enemy wipes out for the time being the opposition and
even criticism of the home government, and unites the most
disparate elements in a common hatred.

This is also the basis of Fichte's patriotism. But the
astonishing thing is that his patriotism did not silence his
criticism of what he considered wrong in the state. Fichte
did not become a Prussian who approved of irresponsible
government. He remained a liberal socialist in domestic
affairs and a "cosmopolite" in international relations.
Under the influence of the times he weds a strong nationalism
with both of these. But his patriotism was entirely too weak
for his contemporaries. He can in no wise be compared
with men like Körner or Ernst Moritz Arndt. Despite his
patriotism he remained a republican and that is undoubtedly
the reason why he was ineffective in his day. If a tag must
be given to the *Reden* they may be described as liberally
nationalist.

The other observation is that the *Reden* are not to be considered as great intellectual masterpieces. Gertrud Bäumer
is right:

The *Reden an die deutsche Nation* are no masterpieces of intellect judged by the standards of scientific thought and
persuasion.[57]

Walz declares that in them the sublime and the grotesque
meet frequently.[58] He denounces their "pedagogical
mania," their "educational despotism," and asks the Germans to cease their ridiculous praise of Fichte as an educa-
tor. It would be an easy task to single out many fundamental ideas of the *Reden* for criticism and even ridicule.
Any sound estimate of the *Reden* will have to recognize
their unscientific character.

[57] *Fichte und sein Werk*, p. 115.
[58] *Op. cit.*, p. 591.

But nationalism does not require sound scholarly ground in order to grow and prosper. Scientific legends make much more fertile soil. And that is precisely the importance of the *Reden* in the history of the development of German nationalism. As they grew more and more isolated from the rest of Fichte's thought and were read as his great and only masterpiece, there was no examination of their scientific soundness, but merely rejoicing at their patriotic fervor.

CHAPTER VI

Doubts and Reaffirmations

1812-1813

Das System der Rechtslehre. 1812

The *Rechtslehre* of 1812 is a restatement with some change of emphasis of the *Grundlage des Naturrechts* of 1796-1797. What these changes are will presently be indicated after the treatise has been summarized.

As basic to his argument, Fichte makes a distinction between Law and Ethics, claiming to be the first to do so, and another distinction between Law and Natural Law.[1] He defines Law as the expression of the general will, and maintains that it functions in the various contracts by which the state is established and secured. The Law is backed by power, enforcing the property contract and the social compact.

Fichte again goes over the field of these contracts and their establishment by the free will of all. Property is not ownership of a thing, but the right to use it. Every one must have such property, or else one has not received justice. That is part of the work of the state. Workers divide into producers, manufacturers, and merchants [2] (*der producirende Stand, der verarbeitende Stand, der Kaufmannsstand*).

As standard of value for prices we again find the bushel of grain. The state can best control this by taking over all

[1] *Nachgelassene Werke*, vol. ii, pp. 495-503.
[2] *Op. cit.*, pp. 544-558.

trade itself.[3] As for money based on this standard, it is best made of paper or leather in a form hard to imitate by forgers. The state is isolated commercially. Foreign commerce is carried on by the state until economic self-sufficiency has been achieved. Property in lands, mines, etc. is not heritable. The state redistributes it after the death of the worker. Other property, such as money, tools, etc. is in reality *res nullius* and falls to the state. But when there is a family it is best that this kind of property revert to the family.[4] A last will or testament is wholly arbitrary and it depends on the will of the community what disposition is to be made of it.

After a longer section on the penal code,[5] Fichte discusses the constitution of the state. The state cannot exist without absolute sovereignty. In order to exercise sovereignty, power must be delegated to certain persons. A pure democracy is no government at all. Hereditary monarchy is too dangerous. The chief thing is a strong *pouvoir exécutif,* which can enforce its will. A separation of function is impossible. A *pouvoir exécutif* might legislate to the end of days and be ineffective. While formerly he advocated a body of ephors as a check on the executive, he decides against it here.[6] Ephors would be suppressed by the executive if troublesome.

In theory the judgment of the people is correct, because there is no higher judge. But what of practice? One can trust a select group of wise men far more than a majority which was constituted God knows how.[7]

[3] *Op. cit.,* p. 568.
[4] *Op. cit.,* p. 602 *et seq.*
[5] *Op. cit.,* pp. 606-627.
[6] *Op. cit.,* pp. 632 *et seq.*
[7] *Op. cit.,* p. 633.

An informed public opinion takes the place of the Ephors. Action by the entire people or revolutions will be found to be evil rather than good. Law and justice should rule the state and all will be well.

The treatise closes with a section on international law (*Völkerrecht*). This is based on absolute outer sovereignty, each nation recognizing the right of existence of all others. A violation of this rule leads to war, which is legally justified. A league of nations, not an international state, will help to regulate the relations between states.

The difference between this treatise and that of 1796 lies largely in the new orientation. That of 1796 started with the individual; this discussion begins with the group. The closed commercial state and all that it implies is here included. The state has compulsive powers, but must exercise these in the interest of freedom and justice. In government the separation of functions is rejected; the executive remains supreme. The Ephors are also put aside. The " general will " is recognized in theory, but in practice delegation of power to the wise is advocated. The best should rule. In foreign politics Machiavellianism, that is, international chaos and attendant distrust of other nations, is dominant. A league of nations provides the only way out.

Aus dem Entwurfe zu einer politischen Schrift im Frühlinge 1813

These pages were written immediately after the famous appeal of the Prussian king to his people (*Aufruf an mein Volk*) on March 17, 1813. Their purpose was merely the clarification of Fichte's thought as to the contemporary situation and his appraisal of the *Aufruf*. The document is in the form of short notes, flashes of thought, that bear on the topic. Since it was not intended for publication in this form, it is all the more revealing as to Fichte's attitude at the height of Prussia's patriotic fervor and activity.

He states that his purpose is to make the people politically free, but the people neither want nor understand freedom. It would be impolitic at present to stir up action against the mighty, but it is all the more necessary to urge the educated to assert their rights at least theoretically.

All monarchic will and monarchic rule must be done away with. The general will must rule. Does the *Aufruf* contain any such promise, or are the free people to be asked to fight in order to keep the chains clamped on themselves? Is the present war a people's war or merely one of the monarch? What is a people's war? What are the aims of the people?

There will never be a German people unless the princes abdicate. Heredity as a governmental principle is against Reason. A united German people may be built only on political freedom. Other factors may help. Thus a war fought together against a common enemy may create a people. A governmental decree can never do so.

What then is a people's war? Certainly not one which merely restores former conditions of government. To give tribute and soldiers to a monarch, what is that but slavery! A real people's war must be in the people's interest, not for the ruler's benefit. And the people's interests are best served by a republican form of government and a constitution. But that is not to be expected from the present war. The German princes will be restored, and inner peace is the best outcome that can reasonably be hoped for. In regard to foreign politics, the only hope is for Prussia to take the lead and move toward a German Reich.

The constitution of the Reich will be extremely important. All citizens are equal; they will receive a common education and receive their places in the state according to their abilities. The Reich is lord of all lands, which it gives out to the tillers of the soil as a loan. All commerce is a monopoly of the state.

As to the nobility and the princes, they must grant true freedom to release their subjects. The false education of princes in the past has created the present evils.

In religion a new state religion will come into being. The state has primacy over the church, and while various churches may continue to exist, the state religion is all-pervading.

In the state, law must prevail over everything else. Whoever is bound by law is a citizen; whoever is forced by compulsion is a subject. The citizens submit to the law because they themselves are the source of it. On the other hand, " the usual fidelity of nobles, loyalty to an overlord, is the virtue of a dog." [8] In this the educated classes have been the worst sinners.

These general principles are then critically applied to the *Aufruf*. Fichte lingers over the idea of a united German people. What a pity if there should never be a German nation! There is a distinct German character. In other nations, national character has been formed by their history, but the Germans have no history in the last centuries. Their character is original. Germans must be careful as to the form of their union. There is a vast difference between confederation and unity. Confederation would be in the interest of the princes.

Common history is a great factor in producing a people and a national character. National honor, pride, and vanity all serve as a tie. Germans have no national honor, but there is a Prussian honor, a Saxon honor, etc.

Have you ever heard a student of Leipzig, a scholar of Berlin from the period of the *Aufklärung*, a Prussian recruiting sergeant, or an Austrian corporal say: Our Kaiser? All this is fanatical peasant pride, and this circumstance more than any

[8] *Werke*, vol. vii, p. 561.

other has denationalized the hearts of the Germans. . . . Today the prince with his splendid court, his honor and external dignity —or whatever it may be—all serve to arouse vanity. Vanity even over resplendent chains of slavery. Whoever wants to be proud will always find cause, even the lowly peasant in his leather pants.[9]

But the Germans have little cause to be proud of their history, or of their literature either. Their literature is read only by the educated few, and these often prefer French and English works. History and literature, then, are not bases of German unity. German unity is a great hope, a great faith. The peculiar and distinctive feature of German national character is the fact that it exists without a state and above the state in purely intellectual development.

Wherefore the great Germans have always found their country too small and have traveled and lived abroad. Consider Leibnitz, Goethe, Schiller, Schlegel, the great teachers at the German universities—Kant alone excepted. Abroad they found the spirit of magnanimity, humanity, gallantry, fortitude. All these were originally German traits and have been acquired from the Germans. The German always seeks a higher universality, but at present he can develop this only abroad. After all, then, what is the difference whether a French marshal like Bernadotte, before whose spirit there had once floated the enthusiastic spirit of liberty, rules a Germanic country instead of an " arrogant German noble without moral principles but with coarse and impudent haughtiness "? If German unity is worth achieving it must be achieved through the freedom of the citizen without sacrificing the majority of the people to slavery and through the equality of all according to the Rights of Man. It can be achieved " only by Germans who have existed for millennia

[9] *Werke*, vol. vii, p. 568.

for this very purpose and are slowly ripening for their mission." There is no other element in mankind for such a development." [10]

The only comment necessary on this remarkable document is the note that Fichte's patriotism is liberal and republican even in the most enthusiastic national atmosphere. There is no need to grow even mildly excited over a war which promises only to restore the *status quo* and to re-establish the authority of the unenlightened German princes and their irresponsible rule.

Die Staatslehre, oder Über das Verhältnis des Urstaates zum Vernunftreiche. 1813

These lectures bear a title which is not Fichte's but which was rather badly chosen by his son and editor. Medicus, editor of another (incomplete) Fichte edition, entitled them *Vorträge verschiedenen Inhalts aus der angewandten Philosophie.* This is more accurate and has the additional merit of being Fichte's own description in his Introduction.[11] After a lengthy introductory statement as to the philosophic basis of his lecture we come to a section called *Über den Begriff des wahrhaften Krieges.*

The highest thing in the world is human life. In order to preserve human life, property came into being. The means to protect property is the state. Ruling families often fight for the privilege of protecting property in states. When such fighting occurs, it is generally carried on by mercenaries, and is strictly an affair of the ruling families. When a conquering family comes into possession of another land and establishes security there, then " quiet is the first duty of the citizen " (*Ruhe is die erste Bürgerpflicht*). Let him be neutral, barricade his door and await with a good

[10] *Werke*, vol. vii, p. 573.
[11] *Werke*, vol. iv, p. 369.

stock of white bread, fresh meat and strong wine that one who will be victor and his future protector. Otherwise he would endanger his life and his property. All considerations, such as the divine ordinance of kings, the sanctity of oaths, national honor, and other relics from barbarous times, mean nothing, because first comes life, then property, and finally the state.

In such sarcastic fashion Fichte disposes of economic liberalism and absolute monarchy. Where the idea of the economically liberal state prevails, wars concern nobody but the rulers.

The philosophic basis of the state is wholly different. Life is a means to moral endeavor and action, whose end is the freedom of all. This is brought about through the state. When a war occurs, it is a threat to the freedom of all, and all are vitally interested and concerned. Every effort must be put forth, the battle must be waged to death, no peace must be concluded without complete victory, otherwise freedom will not be preserved. Let no ruler flatter himself that he has subjects whom he may rule as he will. No ruler is a god, no ruler stands before the fatherland. This is understood by the rulers in the present instance. They do not propose to defend merely a ruling family. They must be trusted.

But if despite that, it should later develop that they were not sincere; if the victory in battle should only serve to sacrifice the independence of the nation to the advantage of the ruling family; if it should be shown that the ruler was willing to have the noblest blood flow for the advantage of his personal rule, and will not dare to jeopardize his government for the independence of his people: then a reasonable man could under no circumstances remain under such a ruler. His activity in society has the sole purpose of sowing the seeds of a free and lawful constitution in society and he may nourish this hope as long as general ignorance is the cause of its non-adoption. But where a longing for freedom and independence has been clearly expressed and yet rejected with open eyes and degraded to a means of slavery; where national characteristics, the postulates of development, are chained by foreign fetters: he has nothing to hope for. Such a state is suffering from a hardening of the heart and has publicly branded itself as a reprobate. Every noble person will rescue his immortal soul and flee from it.[12]

In regard to the present situation it is wrong to depreciate the strength and the resources of the enemy; it is just as foolish to think of the enemy as an instrument in the hand of God. In regard to the latter, God is the very essence of freedom and He would not be identified with the very embodiment of evil, with the kingdom of the devil. The French have never understood, nor can they, the essence of freedom and government under law. The Germans can, and they strive for independence from princes, for the unity of Germany, for freedom based on equality. There is no other element in the world to bring about this development of mankind.

And now look at the man at the head of the enemy. He is no Frenchman and he lacks the best that was in even the worst of French despots like Louis XIV. He came from a wild and ferocious people who fought to break the fetters of slavery. He was educated in France and could have learned that the French people are very pliable and versatile, though lacking in stability. He never learned the moral purpose of life.

Equipped with human greatness, a calm clarity and a firm will, as he was, he might have become the benefactor and liberator of mankind, if only the slightest notion of the moral purpose of man had entered his mind.[18]

[12] *Werke*, vol. iv, pp. 414-415.

[13] *Werke*, vol. iv, p. 425.

But that did not happen and so he stands as a warning example for all mankind. The philosophy of life which he developed was that of a stagnant and warring mankind, to which now and then direction was given by great personalities, such as Charlemagne and himself. This was the only manifestation of the divine in his life and all else must be sacrificed to it—freedom, pleasure, life itself. He evolved plans for ruling the world and perpetuating his rule in a dynasty founded by himself. He is different from other rulers, in that he sees himself as the embodiment of a universal will. His thought is sublime, because it is daring and it rejects all pleasure. What a pity that he uses his strength for the suppression of freedom.

As a vulture hovers in the air and looks about for its prey, so he hovers over stunned Europe, watching for every false move and weakness in order that he may hurl himself down and take advantage of it.[14]

How his clarity of perception differs from that of other rulers! And similarly his strength.

He risks his life and refuses life's comforts; he exposes himself to the heat and frost and to the rain of bullets. He will not give thought to any deterring treaties when they are offered to him. He will not be a peaceful ruler of the world. And if he cannot be that, he would rather be nothing.[15]

If he is to be defeated, he must be opposed by a stronger will and enthusiasm. There are those who see in him a bloody tyrant, who point to his assassination of d'Enghien, but he is guilty of a greater crime than that. He came to the French people when they were struggling for freedom and had shed much blood in the battle for it. Perhaps the

[14] *Werke*, vol. iv, p. 427.
[15] *Ibidem.*

nation was not capable of freedom. But he himself had seen visions of freedom and might have educated the French to it, through his leadership and through a system of national education. Instead of that he cheated the French out of the freedom they had won, because he had not a spark of real understanding.

This was Fichte's famous characterization of Napoleon.

The next section deals *Von der Errichtung des Vernunftreiches*.[16] It moves in the well-known Fichtean circle of ideas: the need of freedom for all, the establishment of the state for that purpose, the rule of law, the need of force in government, the need of a national system of education based on Pestalozzi's ideas, the divine government of the world, the nature of marriage, language as the basis of a nation, etc. It contains no new ideas.

The two following sections, *Alte Welt* and *Neue Welt* [17] hark back to ideas expressed and developed in the *Grundzüge des gegenwärtigen Zeitalters*. State and society in the Old World are characterized by absolutism in government, belief in authority, national gods and theocracies, tribal divisions, inequality and insecurity, evolving gradually through the work of great men and geniuses to ordered society. The New World was made primarily by Christianity. It implied all the opposites of the Old, above all freedom and human rights.

The last essay is remarkable for its almost complete immersion in religion which approaches chiliasm. It very seldom touches the ground or gets close to the realities of history or politics.

[16] *Werke*, vol. iv, pp. 431-496.
[17] *Werke*, vol. iv, pp. 497-520, 521-600.

CHAPTER VII

FICHTE'S NATIONALISM

FICHTE'S Germany was a geographical expression. It was split up into a host of kingdoms, provinces, and principalities each of which claimed sovereignty and the loyalty of its subjects. What devotion there was to one's native land was restricted to these various sections. This was particularism.

As compensation for the lack of a larger national loyalty, German intellectuals had taken the world to their heart. Humanity was their love. What did terms like Prussian, Bavarian, Hessian, or Saxon mean when they were included in the term mankind? And this was also true of terms like Germans, French, Russians, or English. This was cosmopolitanism.

Typical examples of this spirit will illustrate the situation. In a review of J. von Sonnenfels' *Über die Liebe des Vaterlandes*, Goethe wrote in 1772:

The eternal captious plaints are here reiterated: "We have no fatherland, no patriotism." If we find a place in the world where we may rest with our possessions, an acre that will supply us with food, a house that will protect us, do we not then have a fatherland? And do not thousands upon thousands have these in every state? And are we not happy within these limits? Why then the useless striving for a sentiment which is not within the possibilities or even desirable, which with certain peoples at certain times was and is the result of many happily converging incidents? Roman patriotism! May God protect us from this. We should find no chair on which to sit, no bed in which to lie.

To Jakobi he wrote:

According to the flesh let us be and remain citizens of our times, because anything else is impossible; but according to the spirit it is the privilege and duty of the philosopher and of the poet to belong to no nation and to no time, but rather to be a contemporary of all times.

Schiller declared that patriotism is only for immature peoples, for the youth of nations. Lessing announced: " Patriotism is a sentiment which I do not understand. It is, as it seems to me, an heroic infirmity which I am most happy in not sharing." Wieland said that what the Greeks and Romans called patriotism was a passion incompatible with cosmopolitan principles. He further claimed that in his childhood he had been told much about his duties to God and his neighbor, now and then about his duties to his government, but nothing at all about the duties of a German patriot. He could not recall that in his youth he had ever heard the word " German " mentioned respectfully.[1]

Görres rejoiced when Mainz fell into the hands of the French in 1797 and wrote:

On December 30, 1797, on the day when Mainz changed hands, at three o'clock of the afternoon, there died at Regensburg at the ripe old age of 955 years, 5 months, and 28 days quietly and blissfully, in complete exhaustion and paralysis, the Holy Roman Empire of unhappy memory. O God, why did you have to pour out the vials of your wrath over this kindly creature? It was grazing so harmlessly and contentedly on the pastures of its fathers; like a good sheep, it permitted itself to be shorn ten

---

[1] For these examples see Wenck, *Deutschland vor hundert Jahren;* R. Strecker, *Die Anfänge von Fichtes Staatsphilosophie,* pp. 1-19; H. Johnsen, *Das Staatsideal J. G. Fichtes,* pp. 11, 15, 16.

times a year, was always so peaceful and patient; like that despised long-eared beast of burden, it grew unruly and kicked only when mischievous lads burned its ears with red hot coals or rubbed turpentine into its skin.[2]

If these expressions seem strange, it must be remembered that there was no German fatherland at that time. In general, patriotism meant loyalty to a petty princeling with ridiculous pretensions who obviously could claim little importance in larger affairs. The intellectuals believed that their devotion to spiritual matters and to humanity was an ideal that transcended all political categories.

Fichte grew up in this atmosphere. His earliest recorded attitudes are thoroughly in harmony with the prevalent spirit of local patriotism. He had been born and educated in Saxony and he felt gratitude and loyalty for his Saxon homeland. In 1780 he applied for a position as preacher in Saxony. To him this seemed a position not only personally agreeable, but one which would enable him to repay Saxony for what she had done for him. Accordingly he wrote to the government: "If you will grant my petition, I assure you by all that is holy, that I shall be faithful in my office and shall devote myself entirely to my fatherland which assisted me at school and which I have learned to love." Later he wrote on the same matter: "Fatherland is no empty phrase to me. I believe that it is against God's will to withdraw from the state in which he gave us birth as long as this state wishes to make use of our services. I look upon you as the representative of the fatherland."

This is local patriotism pure and unadulterated—*Schollen-patriotismus*—ordinary *Heimatsliebe*. The great world has not yet opened up to him. He was familiar with Saxony and was loyal to it. Fichte began to travel, when no pas-

---

[2] Scherr, *Deutsche Kultur und Sittengeschichte*, p. 524 *et seq.*

torate could be found for him in Saxony. He spent a number of years in various parts of Germany and in Switzerland and Poland. Then only did he learn what a petty
thing his local patriotism had been and how exalted was the
ideal of cosmopolitanism. No special incident or time at-
taches to this conversion. Cosmopolitanism was in the air
and was inescapable for any intelligent German. The
records of those years in Fichte's life are scanty and his
literary plans embracing ambitious projects were never exe-
cuted. One thing is certain—the Fichte that emerges in the
early 1790's is a good cosmopolitan.

A curious item has survived from the year 1790. It is a
short fragment called *Zuruf an die Bewohner der Preussischen Staaten* in which Fichte endeavors to justify the
Prussian censorship. He tries to show that he is a dis-
interested outsider, who reasons calmly with the Prussian
people, on the basis of common sense and fairness. He
says: " Prussia's king is as alien to me as any monarch of
the earth; I respect in him nothing except the great and
good man. I am a foreigner . . . for a short period a
guest in the Prussian states." Interesting that a Saxon
considered himself a " foreigner " in Prussia, and not a
word is mentioned that both are Germans.

About this time Fichte came under the influence of the
ideas and achievements of the French Revolution. His first
response was a vehement protest against irresponsible, absolute government. His two pamphlets of 1792 against Prussian censorship and in defense of the French Revolution are
of this character. There is no understanding of nationalism, there is no appreciation of what the right kind of state
might do for Germany, no ideal of a unified country. Both
pamphlets are anti-state, negative; they deny rights to the
state and claim rights for the people. For this reason,
throughout his pamphlet on the French Revolution he always

refers to "your" state and never to "our" state. He is so little a nationalist that he writes in this same pamphlet:

Do you really believe that the artists or peasants of Germany care in the least whether the artists and peasants of Alsace and Lorraine should henceforth find their city or village in geography textbooks under the chapter Germany, and that they will throw away their spades and other tools to put it there?[3]

But gradually this negative attitude changed, particularly under the influence of the successful deeds of the French nation. Instead of rejecting the state or disdaining to have it intrude on his higher ideals, Fichte began to write treatises on the nature of the state and on its constitution (1796). By 1800 he even envisaged the state as the complete organizer and controller of the entire economic life of the country.

This does not mean that Fichte discarded cosmopolitanism. Far from it. He still clung to the great ideal, but at the same time he felt the need of finding a place for patriotism. He wrestled with this problem in his lectures to the Free Masons and worked out a solution that satisfied him. It is not correct to say with Windelband that his patriotism and cosmopolitanism are as one twin to another. Otto Braun gives a far more satisfactory interpretation, that it is a synthesis toward a higher unity.[4] Fichte recognizes the state and the nation as necessary, even valuable; adherence to it becomes a duty, and the privilege of dissociation of disaffected individuals is abrogated. In the *Closed Commercial State* the state is of enormous importance to the individual. But behind and above the nation is the cosmos,

[3] *Op. cit.*, chap. 3.

[4] Otto Braun, *Johann Gottlieb Fichte, Volk und Staat*, pp. xvii and xviii. Hans Scholz, "Fichte und Napoleon," in *Preussische Jahrbücher*, vol. 152 (1913), p. 5, note, uses the term "konkretisierter Kosmopolitismus."

humanity, and this is what the nation strives for, this is its goal.

The synthesis of patriotism and cosmopolitanism is best understood when we consider the modifications which both undergo in this union. Patriotism is not narrow or exclusive. Even in the *Reden* and in the discussion of the national church, where the approach to chauvinism is closest, there is a strong universal element. Patriotism is not unethical. The purpose of the state is the moral development of mankind. In its inner policy it is bound by various contracts which make for freedom. In its foreign relations it lives in a system of political anarchy in which might prevails. But might is not right. Economic imperialism is robbery. A League of Nations is advocated as an aid to end this international anarchy.

Patriotism, further, does not exclude criticism. Quite the contrary, sound criticism is an act of patriotism. If government is lazy, irresponsible, cowardly, weak, stupid, inattentive to its duties, and corrupt, it deserves the denunciation of a true patriot. Patriotism is therefore not the acceptance of the *status quo*. Unenlightened monarchical government which is based on selfishness must be abolished and in its place a republic must be established. A higher unity is desirable, rather than German provincialism and particularism. Moreover, a German is not always right and a foreigner always wrong. Fichte is willing that a foreigner like Bernadotte be allowed to rule in a Germanic country if he respects the liberties of the people. His opposition to Napoleon is based not on national, but on moral, grounds.

The most important modification of patriotism by cosmopolitanism lies in the fact that it makes cultural values supreme for the nation. The cultural purpose of the state is greater than the political, although the cultural purpose cannot be achieved without the state. What binds people together into a nation? What makes them know and feel that they are Germans? Language and culture. By great emphasis on the language and by exaggerated praise of the pre-eminence of German, Fichte placed language in the foreground of nationalism. And closely allied with it is the culture, the civilization, the literature of a nation. These are the real ties which constitute a sense of belonging together. Other matters also have their degree of importance, such as a common country, a common government, etc., but these are not as important as the former. A nation is possible where there is common culture and political division, while political unity does not necessarily constitute a nation.[4a]

Finally, Fichte's nationalism was ideal. It embraced a country which did not exist except as a hope, that is, an idealized, united Germany. For such an ideal country he envisaged a new government, a new nation, new national traits. Yet his patriotism was real enough. It was devoted to the German language and literature. It was attached to the physical territory of Germany. It demanded a strong army for the protection of the country. Above all, however, it remained a faith in, a hope for, and a sincere devotion to, a future realization. Fichte is merely a lukewarm patriot in relation to the Germany of his day, but he is an enthusiastic patriot in relation to the Germany which is to be.

Turning to cosmopolitanism, we find that it, in turn, is modified by nationalism. The complete indifference toward political matters, so characteristic of cosmopolites, can hardly exist where there is such an interest in the nation

[4a] In view of the latest manifestations of nationalism in Germany (the Hitler movement), it is well to note that Fichte did not consider " racial purity " possible or necessary to German national unity. See especially the *Reden*. Lect. 4.

and the state, as there was in Fichte. Complete submergence in cultural universality is, indeed, foreign to
Fichte's thought. Nations and states existed and had to be
reckoned with. And there was no reason why these nations
should always be isolated or even hostile toward each other.
He proposed a League of Nations, which in essence did no
more than create a balance of power. But the very idea
of a League of Nations is a far cry from dyed-in-the-wool
cosmopolitanism.

Thus we may summarize this synthesis of patriotism and
cosmopolitanism by saying that Fichte's cosmopolitanism
created a cultural-Jacobin nationalism, while his patriotism
produced an embryonic internationalism.

In all essentials Fichte based his ideas of nationalism on
Jacobin nationalism, and he adapted these ideas to German
conditions. It is not at all surprising that the man who
learned the doctrines of natural law and social contracts
from Rousseau, who learned about " constitutions, government, manners, climate, religion, and commerce," from
Montesquieu, about agriculture and the producing classes
from the Physiocrats, and who gained a vision of the new
society from the events of the French Revolution, it is not
at all surprising that this man should lean heavily on the
Jacobins for his doctrine of nationalism.

The Jacobin doctrine of nationalism began with a vague
cosmopolitanism, positing the equality of all men of all
nations. The events of the Revolution, however, compelled
them to apply themselves to the problems of their own
country and the result was that they became patriots also.
For France they demanded a unified nation-state within its
" natural " frontiers; its government was to be a republic;
the privileges of feudal classes and of the clergy were to be
abolished; the administration was to be efficiently centralized; the church was to be removed from all participation in

government, subordinated to the state, and government was to be wholly secular; the nation was to speak French, the *langue républicaine,* which would break down provincial barriers and establish a cultural unity. Finally, this devotion to the nation was raised to the level of a religious cult with its own ritual, saints, days of worship, symbols, etc.[15]

Fichte's nationalism is a translation into German of this French phenomenon. The difference lies chiefly in the fact that much of this program was unrealizable under German conditions. For Fichte it came to be a Great Hope, a Great Goal. At times, particularly in 1807 and 1808, this hope was so strong, his goal seemed so near, that he had a real " experience " of the German nation, even though it did not exist. His faith in this Germany of his dreams can be compared only with Dostoevski's mystical belief in Russia. But Fichte's Germany-that-was-to-be was built along distinctly Jacobin lines. It was not a country in which a down-trodden people was enslaved by arrogant and ignorant princes, in which the clergy held privileged positions and ruled in their " ancient darkness," in which patriotic narrowness and particularism made a travesty of the high mission to the world confided to this people. No, never—even if the country were unified under a powerful monarch and held a respected position in the concert of nations, this could not be. Such a Germany would be a denial of all that Fichte valued, a hollow shell, mere sounding brass and tinkling cymbal. The Germany of the future was to be a republic of free people, ruled by wise and intelligent men of its own choice, unified in government, in culture, in language, eager to perform its duty to the rest of mankind, and throbbing with pride and joy in the knowledge of national greatness.

[5] Crane Brinton, *The Jacobins,* pp. 141-154; Walz, *op. cit.,* chap. 4, " Die Jakobiner," pp. 398-451; Hayes, *The Historical Evolution of Modern Nationalism,* chap. 3.

That explains why the greatest enthusiasm and exultation in Fichte frequently alternated with the deepest anguish and the blackest pessimism. True, things were happening, particularly in Prussia. Stein was freeing the serfs, Hardenberg was reorganizing the administration, Scharnhorst was remaking the army, and Wilhelm von Humboldt was busy with education; yet there was abundant evidence to show that nothing fundamental would be accomplished. The king of Prussia appealed to his people against the foreign aggressor, and his people responded with enthusiasm; but the appeal and the response showed that neither understood Fichte's Great Dream. No doubt the foreigner would be expelled and his power broken. He deserved it; he had betrayed the divine in himself by his selfishness. But after that, what? All signs pointed to a return to the *status quo ante* with minor modifications.

To summarize, by 1800 Fichte had defined for himself a German national program based on Jacobin nationalism. In 1807-1808 this program seemed well within the range of the possible, and he was carried off his feet by the vista that unfolded before him. Yet after a glimpse of that vision, sober reflection made him see how far off was realization. In hopes mingled with doubt and mistrust, the curtain was rung down on his career prematurely, and he was spared the bitter disappointment of witnessing the Holy Alliance and the Metternich system.

This analysis is in itself sufficient to show the error in the traditional view which draws a sharp line of division between nationalism and cosmopolitanism in Fichte marked by the year 1806-1807. Suffice it here to add Léon's summary:

[After 1806] a new Fichte seems to appear: an intemperate realist, a disciple of Machiavelli, a political pamphleteer, a patriotic orator, a combative administrator, eager only for the salvation of the German people by furthering their moral regeneration. But this new Fichte is only an illusion. In reality it is always the same Fichte: the impenitent idealist, the impenitent rationalist, the impenitent revolutionary, applying his ideas and his actions to the tragic circumstances of the age, justifying the Moral Ideas of his Theory of Science by its practical efficacy, prophesying the liberation of Germany by the overthrow of all kings and the advent of democracy.[6]

One other question remains for brief consideration: Fichte's place in the history and development of German nationalism. Fichte lived in an age of transition. At the turn of the century great changes were taking place in German thought and the ideas regarding the state did not escape change either. The German heavens were filled with a galaxy of stars: Kant, Wilhelm von Humboldt, Schelling, Steffens, the Schlegels, Novalis, Tieck, Schleiermacher, Adam Mueller, Kleist, Hegel, and many others. Of these Fichte was by no means the least.

This was also the period of transition from *Weltbürgertum* to nationalism. These two philosophies lived side by side. But the star of nationalism was rising and that of cosmopolitanism was setting.

In Germany this whole situation was strongly colored by the political situation. To some extent Cosmopolitanism was born of political and national impotence. It was a sublimation of political ineptitude, a flight to the Ideal when the Real proved intolerable. It was deeply rooted in German thought, because Germany had for so long been torn to shreds by provincialism. In Germany then, Nationalism could only exist as a hope. There was Prussia, to be sure, stretching ever further across the north German plain.

[6] Léon, *op. cit.*, vol. ii, p. 519.

Napoleon, too, had been very helpful by reducing the several hundred provinces to thirty-eight.

With these beginnings and the great national stir which the French Revolution was creating throughout Europe, Germany was also affected by nationalism. But the men who were influenced by the new spirit could only serve as prophets in Germany. They could point to the goal and inspire the Germans to strive for it. The realization, however, still lay many decades in the future. Fichte was among these prophets. He preached German national unity in season and out of season. More than that, he tied a definite program or constitution to his nationalism, above all, republicanism, socialism, and a touch of internationalism. These were not mere out-lying decorative fringes, but they were part of and in the very center of the picture. Discard these and Fichte would undoubtedly have lost his enthusiasm for the German nation; include these and he could grow lyric about its great possibilities.

Fichte was, then, one of the founders of modern German nationalism. But what of his relationship to later German "integral" nationalism, which became so repellent to the rest of the world? The problem is by no means solved by using such terms as chauvinist, Pan-German, imperialist, and militarist in connection with the later school of thought and in this way absolve Fichte of any fault for their existence. Even the most rabid nationalists use idealistic language. They do not speak of militarism, but of armies for the defense and protection of the Fatherland. "Imperialism" merely means spreading the blessings of civilization to backward peoples. And so on, *ad infinitum et ad nauseam.*

Now there can be no question that in many cases the language of the later integral nationalists is identical with that of Fichte. Bernhardi, for instance, agrees with Fichte specifically that the state is " an exponent of liberty to the human race, whose task is to put into practice the moral duty on earth." [7]   Pan-Germanism, likewise, rests partly on the same racial and linguistic basis about which Fichte was so eloquent.   Finally it cannot be denied that there are extremely, almost grotesquely, nationalist statements in Fichte.

Does that mean that there is no difference between, say, Bernhardi and Fichte?   I think not.   The difference is evident when the totality of thought and work of the two is considered.   Taken as a whole, Fichte and Bernhardi show great unlikeness.   There are elements in Fichte which, though by no means anti-national, are still very objectionable to rabid nationalists intent on continuing the isolationist, monarchical, and capitalist *status quo*.   That explains the persistent avoidance by these groups of vast areas of Fichtean ideas, and the reinterpretation of others.[8] There are in Fichte many convenient pegs on which rabid nationalists may hang their preachments.   But there are even more elements which are anathema to the latter group.

Fichte is one of the prophets of German Nationalism. He has influenced the growth of the national movement in Germany.   But the revolutionary Fichte, the republican Fichte, the socialist Fichte, the Jacobin Fichte, who was the heart and soul of the nationalist Fichte, has been conveniently obliterated.   Later nationalists dressed him up to suit their needs and presented him in this borrowed finery, but very few of them understood the real man behind the mask.

[7] *Germany and the Next War*, p. 25.

[8] The explanation may also lie in their knowledge of nothing but the *Reden* and a misreading of these.

CHAPTER VIII

FICHTE IN THE NINETEENTH AND TWENTIETH CENTURIES

IN tracing the history of Fichte in the century after his death down to the present, it will be convenient to divide the study into three periods: I. 1814-1840; II. 1840-1914; III. 1914-1930.

I. *1814-1840.* *Fichte in Disrepute as a Liberal and Revolutionary*

The Congress of Vienna was the signal for reaction throughout Europe. Nationalism was not recognized. Germany and Italy remained "geographical expressions." Jacobinism and Liberalism were alike denounced and persecuted. The Metternich System ruled most of Europe with its policy of Intervention wherever any opposition was shown to Legitimacy.

In Germany, the Wartburg Festival of the *Burschenschaften* in 1817 and the political assassinations, particularly that of Kotzebue in 1819, brought on a White Reign of Terror. The *Bundesrat* voted to appoint a committee to examine into the causes of radicalism and to denounce and punish its instigators. This committee had its seat at Mainz and was known as the *Zentraluntersuchungskommission*. It produced numerous reports which named various people as dangerous.

Liberalism and nationalism in Germany survived to about 1820. Thereafter they were driven underground, and thus continued their existence, fostered chiefly by the *Burschen-schaften* and similar groups. These were made up largely of students of practically all Protestant universities. Their motto was *Freiheit, Ehre, Vaterland*. They wore the colors of Lützow's corps — black, red, and gold. They became widely known through the Wartburg Festival, mentioned above, at which a number of reactionary books were " burned at the stake " amid the wild enthusiasm of the students.

But the temper of the country at large was undergoing a radical change. Dominant opinion moved from nationalism and liberalism toward local patriotism, cosmopolitanism, and legitimate monarchy. This attitude continued throughout the 1820's and the 1830's.[1]

It is easy to imagine what would happen to Fichte in a period like this. Even then, to be sure, he had some disciples. Speculative thinkers and educators were the first to see greatness in Fichte. They were the first to attribute the revival after 1806 to Fichte's stirring addresses. At his death, in 1814, many former enemies repented and praised Fichte highly in their newspaper obituaries. Others continued hostile and remained silent.[2]

We have seen previously[3] that in the 1810's and 1820's Fichte was generally ignored as a factor in the Wars of Liberation and that the leading historians omitted mention of him in their works. But now this silence and neglect was to be changed to open hostility. The *Mainzer Zentraluntersuchungskommission* in 1822 cited Fichte as one of the most dangerous propagandists of revolutionary and repub-

---

[1] See Lamprecht, *Deutsche Geschichte*, vol. iii, no. 3, pp. 505-517; Ilse, *Geschichte der Politischen Untersuchungen* (Frankfurt a/M., 1860), *passim*.

[2] Körner, *op. cit.*, pp. 77, 79.

[3] See page 132.

lican ideas.[4]   The accusation did not go unanswered.   In September, 1822, a German newspaper replied:

Fichte is the name of the man against whom even his bitterest enemies can say nothing which would cast the least blemish on his character, concerning whom all informed persons in Germany have long since agreed that he is rectitude and purity personified.[5]

In 1824 there was further evidence of antagonism.   A new edition of the *Reden* had been prepared and submitted to the Prussian censorship.   Publication was refused, because the book " nourished deceitful and empty phantoms." Ludwig Robert, a patriotic poet who had personally heard Fichte deliver the *Reden,* took up the cudgels for Fichte in an article in which he declared that " it is altogether wrong to think of Fichte and his works as the French clergy think of Voltaire and his works."   He went on to declare that Fichte was not at all a republican, but a great patriot who had enormous respect for the "princes by the grace of God." But the Prussian censorship did not rescind its action.   The second edition of the *Reden* was printed outside of Prussia in Leipzig.[6]

In 1830 Fichte's son, Immanuel Hermann, began his extensive editorial work on his father's life and labors.   He published the first edition of *Fichtes Leben und Literarischer Briefwechsel.*   For such an initial effort at biography there was apparently very little demand, for the second edition did not appear till 1862.   This second edition con-

---

[4] Ilse, *op. cit.,* p. 30; Janson, *Fichtes Reden an die deutsche Nation,* p. 2.

[5] Scherr, *Menschliche Tragikomödie* (Leipzig, 1884), vol. viii, p. 115.

[6] *Fichtes Leben,* vol. i, p. 423 *et seq.*; I. H. Fichte's Introduction to the 1870 edition of the *Reden,* p. xiv.   It should be noted that Fichte's son was not altogether pleased with Robert's defense of his father and protested the attempt to claim him for national reaction.

tained a significant Introduction. It stated that in 1830 Fichte had no honor among his people, but since then the times had changed very much.[7]

In 1834 Fichte's son began publication of the complete edition of his father's works. The *Nachgelassene Werke* in three volumes appeared first. This again was obviously not a publisher's success. The effort was not continued until 1845. The second edition of *Fichtes Leben* again contained a significant note on the reception of this work. The *Jahrbücher für Wissenschaftliche Kritik* refused to review the work, because " the estimate of Fichte was too favorable." [8]

On the other hand, the liberal element remained loyal to Fichte, particularly the *Burschenschaften*. Fichte, to be sure, was not the " father of the Burschenschaften " as frequently alleged. When a preliminary plan of organization had been submitted to him by Friesen and Jahn in 1812, he had denounced the whole idea as "historisch sowie philosophisch unrichtig," as " wahre Undeutschheit und Ausländerei," and dangerous to the country.[9] Nonetheless he became one of the heroes of this group and was pointed to as an ideal to be followed.[10]

II. *Fichte as Nationalist Hero and as Socialist,* *1840-1914*

Reactionary and particularistic as was the period from 1815 to 1840, there were yet signs of a new day. In 1818 Prussia abolished all internal tariffs and by 1833-35 the

[7] *Fichtes Leben*, 2d edition, p. vi.

[8] *Fichtes Leben*, vol. i, p. 170, note.

[9] Hermann Haupt, " Die Jenaische Burschenschaft von der Zeit ihrer Gründung bis zum Wartburgfest," *Quellen und Darstellungen zur Geschichte der Burschenschaften*, vol. i, pp. 18-113.

[10] Henderson, *A Short History of Germany* (New York, 1902), vol. ii, p. 329.

Zollverein was created, which most German states had joined in 1842. Friedrich List also carried on extensive agitation against the thirty-eight different tariffs in Germany.

At the same time the 1830's showed a decided let-up in the anti-national, cosmopolitan, and particularistic trends of thought. Liberalism was growing and becoming more vociferous in its demands for a constitution and for national unity. Great hopes for these ends were placed in the heir apparent of Prussia who ascended the throne in 1840 as Frederick William IV.

All this vague and rather inert sentiment of the time was suddenly crystallized by the French war scare of 1840. French designs in the Near East had brought about common action by the four great powers, Great Britain, Russia, Austria, and Prussia, for the protection of Turkey. This angered Thiers, then at the helm in Paris, and aroused a good deal of nationalist and militarist spirit in France. The immediate answer of France to the opposing European coalition was the demand for the Rhine boundary, but by 1841 Guizot was in control and the danger of war had passed. Thiers' threat, however, left a lasting impression in Germany. As if by magic the Germans were united. Every German became a patriot over night. The " historic enemy " must be repelled. The song writers became active and Becker's *Rheinlied* (" Sie sollen ihn nicht haben den freien deutschen Rhein ") swept the country. More than 150 melodies were composed for this one song. At the same time Max Schneckenburger wrote *Die Wacht am Rhein*, which in 1870 was to become the German national hymn. A host of patriotic poets and orators roused the nation to self-consciousness and action. Lamprecht sees in 1840 the birth year of German nationalism.[11]

[11] *Deutsche Geschichte*, vol. iii, no. 3, pp. 505-517.

From this beginning the national movement went steadily onward, nourished especially by wars. In 1859 the Italian wars kept Germany in constant excitement and Bismarck's sympathies were outspoken for Italy against Austria. In the 1860's the war over Schleswig-Holstein and the war with Austria added new fuel to the patriotic fires which, in 1870-71 in the Franco-Prussian War, burst forth into a huge blaze which burned down the barriers of sectionalism and unified Germany. From 1870 to 1914 nationalism continued to grow, due chiefly to Germany's attempt to secure her " place in the sun " and to the constant friction of the international alliances. Imperialism and " encirclement " never for a minute permitted a diminution in nationalist ardor.

Another current in this period was that of liberalism, which, in general, had as its goal not only national unity but also constitutional monarchy.[2] The first—and virtually the last—significant manifestation of liberalism was in the revolution of 1848. In horror the Prussian king recoiled from a " government by paragraphs," and solemnly swore that " no sheet of written paper shall ever thrust itself like a second Providence between God in Heaven and this land." In spite of these protestations the " sheet of paper " did manage to come between God and the Prussian monarchs. Constitutions were also adopted in most of the other German lands, granting political rights of a sort to the " subjects."

The republican movement never made real headway, but it was not entirely dead. The radicals were virtually the only ones who continued to profess this hopeless cause against the nationally entrenched monarchy.

[12] Jean de Grandvilliers, *Essai sur le libéralisme allemand* (Paris, 1914) ; H. A. L. Fisher, *The Republican Tradition in Europe* (New York, 1911), pp. 250-269.

The second part of the liberal program, national unity, was held in common with practically all other groups and was therefore not distinctive. After 1848 Liberalism as a separate movement virtually ceased to exist, except in the South German states.

A third current in nineteenth-century Germany was Socialism. One of its early leaders was Ferdinand Lassalle. Lassalle was in agreement with Karl Marx on many matters and sought to win for the workingman his just place in the industrial system. Particular strength was added to Lassalle's movement by the fact that it was a national movement. German Social Democracy under Lassalle was interested in Germany. Lassalle himself made proposals about the Prussian constitution in 1862 (*On the Nature of a Constitution*). Thus Socialism under Lassalle could advocate economic changes and still be patriotic. Only after Lassalle's death did the movement become divided between the national and international or even anti-national groups.

It is among the three groups of nationalists, liberals, and socialists that we must seek in Germany after 1840 the development of thought about Fichte.

A. *Fichte and the German Nationalists—1840-1914*

In 1845 Fichte's son completed the editing of his father's works. Eight volumes were added to the three published in 1834. Additional finds of Fichteana continued to be made, but this edition in eleven volumes, together with the two volumes of the Life and Letters, constituted the bulk of Fichte's literary heritage,[13] and made it possible for serious students to study Fichte's place in the history of thought.[14] It also made it possible for nationalists to un-

---

[13] On the character of I. H. Fichte's editing, see *Bibliography*.

[14] By a curious chance Ferdinand Lassalle was employed by Veit und Co., in Berlin, at the time Fichte's collected works were brought out by

cover further material for the creation of a national hero. The Introductions to these various works are at times distinctly nationalist in tone.

In 1846 William Smith published in Boston his *Memoir of Johann Gottlieb Fichte*. The discussion was chiefly about Fichte's metaphysics, but there was a passage about the *Reden* which were described as " famous." Wilhelm Busse's two-volume study of 1848-49, *J. G. Fichte der Philosoph*, was the first lengthy study of Fichte, but except for a rather non-committal statement in the Introduction about the " stirring times," it did not refer to Fichte's importance politically or nationally.

In volume III of his *Deutsche Geschichte*, published in 1856, Ludwig Häusser dwelt at length on Fichte and especially on the *Reden*. Of these he said: " Since Luther, no one has spoken to the German nation like this." [15]

During the excitement of the Italian wars (1859), I. H. Fichte edited another of the many editions of the *Reden*. It was dedicated to " der deutschen Jugend des gegenwärtigen Geschlechts, besonders den vaterländischen Kriegern." [16]

In 1860 Heinrich Schwarz published his *J. G. Fichte, des deutschen Kraftmannes, Lebensweisheit und vaterländische Gedanken*. He treated of Fichte's ethical idealism (*Lebensweisheit*) and then of his patriotism. The second section extolled Fichte as a good, patriotic German.

The same year Zeller published a study on " Johann Gottlieb Fichte als Politiker " in the *Historische Zeitschrift*.[17]

this publisher. It became part of his task to work with this material and Lassalle's thorough knowledge of Fichte which he used strikingly at a later period was thus brought about. See *Herr Julian Schmidt der Literarhistoriker mit Setzerscholien herausgegeben* (Berlin, 1862), p. 47.

[15] *Op. cit.*, pp. 205-212.

[16] *Fichtes Leben*, vol. i, p. 442.

[17] Vol. 4, pp. 1-35.

He described the early Fichte as a thoroughgoing cosmopolite who was converted into an enthusiastic nationalist by the stress of the Napoleonic oppression. He emphasized the great suffering of the Germans at that time and pointed to Fichte's complete conversion to the cause of his people as a triumph of nationalism.

All of these items were merely straws which indicated how the wind was blowing. They were preparatory for the great Fichtean year of 1862. This year marked the hundredth anniversary of Fichte's birth. The occasion was not to pass without considerable celebration. The universities remembered that Fichte had been a famous teacher in his day, that he had written time and again about education, and that he had played a prominent rôle in the founding of the university of Berlin. Fichtean memorial celebrations were held at all the outstanding schools. The learned journals carried articles about Fichte and the newspapers followed suit. Lectures about Fichte were delivered even in the smallest cities, and his work was extolled. When the year had passed, a survey was made by one of the philosophical journals of the various *Festschriften* and they were found to run into scores. The survey itself was very nationalist, and Fichte was portrayed as a " German hero." [18]

Windelband declared in 1890 that all these celebrations were held in honor of the *patriot* Fichte and not the *philosopher*.[19] This was undoubtedly true. The titles cited by Reichlin-Meldegg indicate two things clearly: that the Ger-

---

[18] K. A. v. Reichlin-Meldegg, "Der hundertste Geburtstag Johann Gottlieb Fichtes. Eine übersichtliche Darstellung der Fichte-festschriften," *Zeitschrift für Philosophie und Philosophische Kritik*, vol. 42 (1863), pp. 242-277.

[19] Wilhelm Windelband, *Fichtes Idee des deutschen Staates* (Freiburg, 1890), p. 5.

man patriots were celebrating a great occasion; that the *Reden* were the center of interest and discussion.

There is no need to go into details about this "patriotic orgy." Such speeches, lectures, essays, pamphlets, etc. which are accessible have been examined and are found listed in the *Bibliography*. Only a few of the items deserve special notice.

First, there was von Treitschke's essay on *Fichte und die nationale Idee* published in *Historische und Politische Aufsätze*, vol. I. Treitschke was using Fichte's anniversary as he did that of Uhland and Lessing, for his propaganda for a united German fatherland.[20] It contained the Fichtean picture which has since become traditional. The cosmopolite was moved by the plight of his people under Napoleonic oppression, and amid great danger to himself he roused the German people by the *Reden*, "das edelste seiner Werke," one of the great historic deeds of German history. This event marked Fichte's conversion to nationalism. The interpretation was not new with von Treitschke, but his adoption of it, as well as his inclusion of it in his *History*, was a very important factor in fixing it as a lasting portrait of Fichte.[21]

Another significant address in 1862 was that of Juergen Bona Meyer, *Über Fichtes Reden an die deutsche Nation*. This was the first critical treatment of the *Reden*. Above all, Meyer denied the vast effect of the *Reden* on German national revival. He saw no evidence for such a claim. He denied the importance of the *Reden* in the events following 1806-1807, both on the German people and on the

[20] Guilland, *Modern Germany and Her Historians* (London, 1915), p. 268.

[21] Karl Tschuppik, "Heinrich von Treitschke und die Folgen," *Neue Rundschau*, vol. 42 (1930), pp. 145-159, denies that Treitschke is a child of Fichte and Hegel. He points out the differences between German Idealism and Treitschke.

reform movement. The *Reden* had acquired such a reputation much later. This was suggestive criticism, but it was
not followed up and documented until 1927 by Rudolf
Körner.[22]

Closely allied to Meyer's criticism was the double statement of Lassalle in 1862 on Fichte. The first was in the
nature of an address delivered May 19, 1862 and entitled
*Die Philosophie Fichtes und die Bedeutung des deutschen
Volksgeistes.* This address was partly philosophical, partly
nationalist. Socialism was not even mentioned.[23] Significant of the nationalist Lassalle was his closing sentence:
"On the day on which the bells peal out, in honor of Fichte's
spirit, the birthday of the German state—on that day we
shall celebrate the true Fichte festival." [24] Even the Socialist was contributing to the national legend.

Lassalle's other statement of 1862 was more significant.
The fourth edition of Julian Schmidt's literary history,
Geschichte der deutschen Literatur, had appeared in 1858.
It now fell into Lassalle's hands and he issued a pamphlet
in reply, called *Herr Julian Schmidt der Literarhistoriker
mit Setzer-Scholien herausgegeben.* Schmidt had completely appropriated the national interpretation of Fichte,
and in a rather superior way he had commented on Fichte's
cosmopolitanism and how rapidly it had vanished when
confronted with the realities of the political situation. He
had perceived a great abyss between the *Grundzüge* of 1805
and the *Reden* of 1807-08, and had marvelled that Fichte
himself did not realize the inconsistency of his *Reden*. Lassalle took up the cudgels against this literary historian in a

[22] Rudolf Körner, "Die Wirkungen der Reden Fichtes," in *Forschungen
zur Preussischen und Brandenburgischen Geschichte*, vol. 40, part 1 (1927)
pp. 65-87.

[23] See Walz, *op. cit.*, p. 590.

[24] *Op. cit.*, p. 26.

most brutal and sarcastic manner. He cited a passage from
Schmidt and proceeded to write footnotes to it.[25] Lassalle
dealt with the literary historian as with an ignorant school-
boy. He ridiculed the idea that Fichte was a patriotic
Prussian. He denounced as absurd the idea that there was
a sharp break in Fichte's thought after Jena and that the
Grundzüge and the *Reden* were in sharp contrast. Lassalle
maintained that the ideas of both were essentially the same,
and that the learned professor had merely skimmed his
Fichte. It is also highly significant that Lassalle reserved
some of his keenest satire for Schmidt's contention that
Fichte was "kleindeutsch." Lassalle classified Fichte as
"grossdeutsch."

The year 1862 also produced a full-length study of Fichte
by Ludwig Noack, *Johann Gottlieb Fichte nach seinem
Leben, Lehren und Wirken*, but the political side was not in
the foreground. Simultaneously, further source material
was contributed to Fichtean studies by M. Weinhold, *48
Briefe von J. G. Fichte und seinen Verwandten*, dealing
with the early life of Fichte.

The year 1862 was thus a definite landmark in the emergence of Fichte as a national hero. It did not create the
hero; it was rather the culmination of a quiet development.
But after 1862 there could be no doubt that Fichte counted
among the great national prophets of Germany.

It is needless to pursue in detail the trail that leads to
1914. Fichte has become established in the national Wal-
halla and a detailed bibliography would perhaps be the
easiest way to bring the account up to date. Instead, it will
perhaps be more significant to note some of the outstanding works, especially as they represent deviations or elabora-
tions of the established picture.

In 1865 Gustav Schmoller published an incomplete study

[25] The section dealing with Fichte will be found on pages 47-72.

on Fichte which pressure of work would not permit him to complete, *Johann Gottlieb Fichte. Eine Studie aus dem Gebiete der Ethik und der Nationalökonomie.*[26] It was an examination by a distinguished economist of Fichte's economic program, particularly of *Der Geschlossene Handelsstaat.* Schmoller concluded that Fichte had clearly perceived the real problems of national economics (money, prices, home and foreign markets, etc.), but that he himself could not agree with Fichte's solutions. It will be recalled that Fichte had written the tract on the *Closed Commercial State* as a remedy for Prussia's economic ills and had dedicated it to the Prussian Minister Struensee from whom he expected immediate action. Schmoller's analysis was apparently the first serious consideration of the work.

In 1869 Kuno Fischer wrote his excellent study of Fichte in his *Geschichte der Neueren Philosophie.* Fischer's work included all phases of Fichte's development, his politics as well as his metaphysics. It marked a great advance in scholarly study, though it, too, treated of Fichte as a national hero in the accepted sense.

Another edition of the *Reden* was edited by I. H. Fichte in 1871. Dated " in the first year of the new German Reich," the editor's 38-page Introduction pointed out the " message " of the *Reden* for the new day. Among the matters emphasized is what has become known as Pan-Germanism. Germany cannot rest until it has acquired *full unity*, that is, until the Tyrolese and the other Germans in Austria have been included in the German Empire. The Danube must be a German stream and the Adriatic must be open through Trieste to German penetration.[27] It may be

[26] *Jahrbücher für Nationalökonomie und Statistik,* vol. 5 (1865), pp. 1-61.

[27] *Op. cit.,* p. xviii.

presumed that the editor knew the famous anti-imperialist blast in the *Reden*, but that did not deter him from putting Pan-German ideas into the Introduction.

Leopold von Ranke in his autobiography *Zur eigenen Lebensgeschichte* [28] discussed Fichte in an item dated November, 1885. He declared that Fichte made a very deep impression upon him in his youth, especially the popular and political writings. As to the *Reden*, he admitted: " Den *Reden an die deutsche Nation* widmete ich eine unbegrenzte Bewunderung."

On the occasion of the Kaiser's birthday in 1890, Wilhelm Windelband delivered an address on Fichte. [29] He pointed out that the outstanding characteristic of Fichte's work was its nationalism, that the world citizen of 1804-05 had become a patriot after 1806-07. Finally he ventured a criticism of Fichte, namely that he had underestimated monarchy. Had he been able to foresee the work of the nineteenth-century Hohenzollern he would have changed his opinion. A rather interesting spectacle—the harsh critic of princes and rulers served up on the Kaiser's birthday celebration.

Among the Pan-Germans, Ernest Hasse proposed a closed mid-European commercial area which would be able to compete with all rivals. This may have been an extension of Fichte's idea, but not necessarily so. The idea was expressed by various people, among them Friedrich List and Baron Bruck, Austrian Minister of Commerce, and the area to be included varied, for Bruck's scheme took in the Balkans and the entire Black Sea region. [30]

[28] *Sämtliche Werke* (Leipzig, 1890), vol. 53-54, p. 59.

[29] *Fichtes Idee des deutschen Staates. Rede zur Feier des Kaisers Geburtstages am 27. Januar 1890.*

[30] Mildred Wertheimer, *The Pan-German League* (New York, 1924), pp. 101-102; Eugene Bagger, *Francis Joseph* (New York, 1927), pp. 162-163.

In 1901 Otto Stock published an article under the rather forbidding title, *Johann Gottlieb Fichte als Herold und Vorbild echter Vaterlandsliebe*.[31] Stock declared that Fichte might well be cited against the " externalization of our national consciousness " and against the " inept hurrah patriotism " of our day.[32] He pointed out that Fichtean patriotism would imply emphasis on freedom, religion, spiritual and intellectual values.

In 1903 Washington Gladden delivered the William Belden Noble Lectures at Harvard. The series was published under the title *Witnesses of the Light*. One chapter dealt with " Fichte, the Philosopher." [33] In general Fichte was held up as an exemplary character. His influence in education was stressed. The *Reden* were described as " one of the great events of German history." At the same time, the lecturer issued a warning to the Kaiser that he must heed Fichte and establish democracy in his country.

In 1905 Eduard Spranger undertook to prove a contention which had generally been accepted without proof that after 1806 Fichte had a great influence on reforms in Prussia. He limited himself to Hardenberg's Riga memoir of 1807, which had been inspired and probably worked out by Altenstein.[34] It was a plea for greater democracy in government. Inasmuch as this was not granted, Spranger's argument is somewhat beside the point.

In 1905 appeared Medicus, *J. G. Fichte. 13 Vorlesungen,* one of the best biographies of Fichte.

[31] *Neue Jahrbücher für das klassische Altertum,* vol. viii (1901), pp. 1-10.

[32] " Fortschreitende Veräusserlichung unseres Nationalbewusstseins," " öde Hurrahpatriotismus."

[33] *Op. cit.,* pp. 101-104.

[34] " Altensteins Denkschrift von 1807 und ihre Bezieh ngen zur Philosophie," in *Forschungen zur Brandenburgisch und Preussischen Geschichte,* vol. 18 (1905), pp. 471-517.

In 1906 J. Holland Rose wrote on Fichte in the *Cambridge Modern History*.[35] His account was essentially von Treitschke's of 1862, for he emphasized the *Reden* and interpreted Fichte as an outstanding nationalist. This interpretation had now gone over into historical writing everywhere. The picture in Henderson's *Short History of Germany* of 1903 differed in no wise from Rose's.

Friedrich von Bernhardi, outstanding exponent of militarism and its benefits, mentioned Fichte several times with evident approbation. He saw in him a national hero in the Wars of Liberation and he approved his conception of the State as " an exponent of liberty to the human race." [36]

In 1911-12 Medicus published a new edition of Fichte's *Werke* in six volumes. Some faults of I. H. Fichte's editing were corrected. Although the Medicus edition was not complete, it did place at the disposal of students most of Fichte's works at a time when the earlier edition was more than sixty-five years old and not readily obtainable.

In 1911 Friedrich Janson attempted once again to meet Juergen Bona Meyer's contention that Fichte's *Reden* had had no influence on his times. Janson's study, *Fichtes Reden an die deutsche Nation. Eine Untersuchung ihres aktuell politischen Gehalts*,[37] reaffirmed the influence of the *Reden* with precious little proof. But it went farther. It destroyed the widely accepted break in Fichte's thought after 1806 by declaring that the *Reden* were a continuation of the *Grundzüge*. By explanations of various kinds, it tended to modify many accepted views of Fichte.

The years 1913-14 marked a double anniversary. 1913 was the centenary of the Völkerschlacht at Leipzig and 1914 was the hundredth anniversary of Fichte's death.

[35] Vol. ix, pp. 325-328.

[36] *Germany and the Next War* (New York, 1914), pp. 25, 65.

[37] In *Abhandlungen zur Mittleren und Neueren Geschichte*, no. 33.

Both were commemorated widely in Germany, and again there was an outpouring of addresses and pamphlets. There was nothing new in this literature and it need not detain us. Only one item deserves mention. For the celebration of 1913 Gerhart Hauptmann, the great German poet and novelist, wrote a Festspiel,[38] a sort of pageant, which was enacted at Breslau, and in which Fichte was made to appear and talk at length about the *Reden*.

All through this period, there was a growing literature on Fichte's educational program. Sometimes the national elements were stressed, sometimes the social elements. There was very little criticism of either.

To sum up. Beginning in 1840, and especially through the centenary of 1862, Fichte was treated more and more as a national hero and prophet. Of all his works the *Reden* were chiefly remembered and these were interpreted in any way that happened to suit the immediate needs of the nationalists, not excluding Pan-Germanism and absolute monarchy. The *Reden* were seen as a mighty stroke against Napoleon and to them were ascribed a powerful influence on the reforms after 1806. Moreover, the year 1806-07 was seen as the dividing line between cosmopolitanism and patriotism in Fichte's thought. Finally, this interpretation became the accepted one in standard historical writing.[39]

[38] *Festspiel in deutschen Reimen. Zur Erinnerung an den Geist der Freiheitskriege der Jahre 1813, 1814, 1815. Aufgeführt bei der Jahrhundertfeier in Breslau* (Berlin, 1913).

[39] Nationalist historiography included another characteristic item, namely that the period from 1806 to 1815 was entirely a conflict against a foreign foe and not against the German princes. This is beautifully illustrated by one of Bismarck's first speeches, on May 17, 1848. Bismarck bullies his way through many vehement objections to the unequivocal declaration that the German uprising at the beginning of the century was against " foreign tyranny," not against " internal tyranny." (See *Die politischen Reden des Fuersten Bismarcks*, vol. 1, pp. 8-10.) Such an interpretation permitted the nationalists to glory in the era of " Prussian regeneration " without consideration of its liberal or socialist aspects.

B. *Fichte and the Liberals and Socialists* [40]

The goal of the Liberals—constitutional government— was in the foreground of German politics but once during the nineteenth century. The Revolution of 1848 marked the high water mark of constitutionalist agitation and at the same time its submergence as a movement. Thenceforth, until 1914, monarchism became firmly imbedded in German nationalism, due particularly to the work of Bismarck.

The Forty-Eighters owed some of their ideas and inspiration to Fichte, though it appears that others readily overshadowed him. Liberalism had survived in the *Burschenschaften* whose members were outstanding leaders of the Forty-Eighters. This point was particularly stressed by Carl Schurz.[41] The relation of Fichte to the philosophic background of the Revolution of 1848 was indicated in general terms by several other Liberal writers.[42]

Liberalism receded from the political scene and was partially replaced by Lassalle's Socialism. Lassalle's Socialism, in turn, was pushed into the background by that of Marx and Engels, which eventually yielded to the Revisionism of Bernstein. When Fichte's socialism was remembered, it was generally by Socialists. Occasionally opponents of Socialism referred to Fichte. A few illustrations may indicate the trend.

Lassalle was thoroughly acquainted with Fichte and he

[40] To separate Liberals and Socialists from nationalists is an oversimplification and an artificial division, because both were generally nationalist Liberal and nationalist Socialist. It is done here merely for reasons of convenience and emphasis.

[41] Carl Schurz, *The Reminiscences of Carl Schurz* (3 vols., New York, 1907), vol. i, pp. 109, 110.

[42] Adolf Rapp, *Der deutsche Gedanke. Seine Entwicklung im politischen und geistigen Leben seit dem 18. Jahrhundert* (Bonn, 1920), pp. 145-149; Karl Marx, *Revolution und Kontre-Revolution* (Stuttgart, 1919), "Die Anfänge der liberalen Opposition," pp. 13-25.

wrote about him at least three times. In all of these, with variations, the emphasis was on Fichte's nationalism; in none of them was there any consideration of his socialism. *Fichtes politisches Vermächtnis und die neueste Gegenwart* (1860) was a commentary on Fichte's *Aus dem Entwurf zu einer politischen Schrift im Frühlinge 1813* in which Fichte had remarked bitterly on the *Aufruf an mein Volk* of that year. Fichte had pointed out that the people would gain nothing by supporting monarchical wars and had added a plea for republicanism. This reminder was very much in order after the war scare of 1859.

Lassalle's address in 1862 on the occasion of Fichte's centenary has been noted, as well as his attack on the literary historian, Julian Schmidt. In the first, the emphasis was on Fichte's transcendentalism and nationalism; in the second, on Fichte's republicanism. Socialism was not mentioned in either. All of which was quite in keeping with Lassalle's national socialism. In many of Lassalle's other works Fichte's influence is evident, though not usually acknowledged.

Schmoller's study of 1865, *Johann Gottlieb Fichte. Eine Studie aus dem Gebiete der Ethik und der Nationalökonomie*, discussed previously, centered attention on Fichte's economic program.

In 1878, Jürgen Bona Meyer wrote his *Fichte, Lassalle und der Sozialismus.* He emphasized Fichte's influence on Lassalle and appended many criticisms of Fichte's socialist doctrines. In 1898 Dr. Jodl added another criticism of Fichte's socialism in *J. G. Fichte als Sozialpolitiker.*[43] His emphasis was on Fichte's educational and socialist theories. There was no mention of Fichte's nationalism. Hans Lindau, *Johann Gottlieb Fichtes Lehre von Staat und Gesellschaft in ihrem Verhältnis zum neueren Sozialismus* (1899) was chiefly critical.

[43] *Zeitschrift für Philosophie,* n. s. 112/113 (1898), pp. 191-216.

In 1900 Marianne Weber opened a new phase in the discussion with her *Fichtes Sozialismus und sein Verhältnis zur Marxschen Doktrin*. According to her, Marxism with its class struggle and Fichtean socialism with its ethical activism were obviously quite different. This was increasingly pointed out by writers of various schools, partly with the idea of dissociating themselves from Fichte, and partly with the idea of rescuing Socialism from Marxism. Among these studies may be mentioned Igino Petrone, *Lo stato mercantile chiuso di G. Ama. Fichte e la premessa teorica del comunismo giuridico*; [44] Luigi Perego, *L'idealismo etico di Fichte e il socialismo contemporaneo. Per una religione socialista* (1911),[45] the subtitle of which indicates clearly what the author is seeking; and Carl Trautwein's excellent study of the interrelation or antagonism between Fichtean and Marxian socialism, *Über Ferdinand Lassalle und sein Verhältnis zur Sozialphilosophie* (1913).

There were many other studies of Fichte's socialist and economic doctrines. Mention might be made especially of Glücksohn's *Fichtes Staats- und Wirtschaftslehre*,[46] which traced in detail the derivation and implications of Fichte's economic thought, as well as Max Adler's chapter on Fichte in his *Wegweiser, Studien zur Geistesgeschichte des Sozialismus* (1914).

A curious use of Fichte was made by Hobohm, *Gedanken-*

[44] *Atti della R. Accademia di Scienze Morali e Politiche*, Napoli, vol. 35-36 (1905-06), pp. 391-441.

[45] These various Italian works are explained by a note in *Croce's History of Italy, 1871-1915* (Oxford, 1929). In a chapter on "The advance of culture and spiritual unrest, 1901-1914" this sentence occurs: "Great ideas which had been obscured shone once more with their former brightness, fertile lines of thought were again pursued, courage and zeal for speculation was reborn, the books of the great philosophers both ancient and modern were reopened, including even such special objects of detestation as Fichte and Hegel," p. 238.

[46] *Berner Studien*, vol. 70, 1910.

welt Fichtes. This study appeared in the *Burschenschaft-liche Bücherei,* a series intended to help keep alive the liberal spirit of the Burschenschaften.[47]   Its purpose was to oppose the negative policy of the Social Democrats who were appealing to Fichte for support.   Hobohm believed that an appeal to Fichte implied an active policy.

Finally, mention should be made of Eduard Bernstein, *Wie Fichte und Lassalle national waren.*[48]   This appeared in 1914 and was undoubtedly occasioned by the extravagant claims of the nationalists in 1913 and 1914 on the occasion of the Fichte celebrations.   The leader of the Socialist Revisionists here reverted to Lassalle's criticism and attempted to claim for Fichte a nationalism wholly different from that generally ascribed to him.

This brief survey will help to emphasize the fact that Fichte was remembered as a Socialist in the century after his death.   Socialists discussed his economic doctrines and pointed out his republicanism.   But this current was by no means as deep and wide as was the nationalist interpretation.   To this day many textbooks on Socialism either omit Fichte entirely or give him a sentence or two as forerunner of Lassalle.   Nonetheless the very considerable literature on Fichte's socialism indicates that Fichte the socialist has survived along with Fichte the patriot and nationalist.

III. *1914-1930.   The World War and After*

A double Fichte picture came down to the World War: Fichte the national hero and prophet, and Fichte the republican and socialist.   The first was that of the German nationalists, of most historians in and out of Germany, and of the German people who learned it in their school books.

---

[47] Vol. 2 (1904), pp. 347-396.

[48] *Archiv für die Geschichte des Sozialismus und der Arbeiterbewegung,* vol. 5 (1914), pp. 143-162.

The second was that of the Socialists and had fewer adherents. What happened to Fichte during the World War is an easy guess: the Germans extolled him while the Allies reviled him. We need only fill in the details to see how true this was.

On the German side there were immediate appeals to Fichte for the arousing of patriotic war enthusiasm. Such appeals to Fichte were by no means the worst features of war literature. Direct vituperation and hymns of hate were far more popular and effective. Fichte was invoked, rather, as the prophet of the educated. A few examples will suffice to show the trend. The historian Reincke-Bloch delivered an address which he called *Fichte und der deutsche Geist von 1914*. This was printed and the proceeds were used for war-relief work. There was no mere denunciation in it; it was only a strongly patriotic speech. The same may be said of Max Lenz' study, *Deutsches Nationalempfinden im Zeitalter unserer Klassiker*.[49] Here Fichte appeared as a patriot among many other patriots. Ernst Bergmann, *Fichte als Erzieher zum Deutschtum* was a more ambitious attempt, originating in a lecture delivered in the celebrations of 1913-14. It contained many references to the times.

During the war years Fichte was also used as a peg on which to hang some criticism or some constructive plan. In January, 1917, for instance, an article on Fichte's *Machiavelli* appeared in the *Sueddeutsche Monatshefte* under the title "Fichtes Lehre von der aeusseren Politik."[50] It was apparently intended as a criticism of the weak and vacillating foreign policy of the government, though it achieved this in a roundabout way. The anonymous writer commented rather sharply on the censorship in Fichte's day,

[49] *Jahrbuch der Goethe Gesellschaft*, n. s., vol. 2 (1915).
[50] Vol. 14 (1917), pp. 467-478.

and added that all intelligent people knew why he had assailed the censorship. *Sapienti sat!*

Another Fichtean idea was resurrected during the War: the advocacy of a league of nations. In June, 1918, R. Eberhard recalled " Fichtes Gedanken über einen Völkerbund zur Aufrechterhaltung des Friedens." [51] In a curious hodge-podge of militarism, chauvinism, and war weariness, in which Fichte became " der Philosoph des Weltkrieges " and the *Reden* were characterized as " kriegerisch," the author outlined Fichte's plan for a league of nations by which eternal peace would become possible. He made a special point of the fact that Fichte had opposed secret alliances.

At the same time Fritz Medicus took up the same idea in "J. G. Fichte als Anhänger und Kritiker des Völkerbundgedankens." [52] A league of nations, he said, might guarantee peace and give weight to international law, but its dangers lay in the possibility that the most powerful nations might make the league an instrument of their plans and intrigues and thus virtually constitute might as right and thereby destroy the culture of other nations.

The pacifists also began discussion of Fichte toward the close of the War. A. Siemsen wrote an article on " Der missbrauchte Fichte " in January, 1919.[53] He declared that Fichte was neither an imperialist, a militarist, nor an advocate of Machiavellian a-moral politics, but rather a state socialist and internationalist. Fichte, he said, had been dealt with shamefully during the War, every war-monger claiming his authority for his preachments. What all of them

---

[51] *Preussische Jahrbücher*, vol. 172 (1918), pp. 394-401.

[52] *Zeitschrift für Völkerrecht*, vol. 11 (1918), pp. 141-154.

[53] *Zeitschrift für Völkerfriede*, vol. 19 (1919), pp. 3-4. This was preceded by an article by Jobst in the same journal in 1918 entitled "Fichte und der Pazifismus."

did, in fact, was to leave aside everything in Fichte which did not suit their needs and center their attention on isolated passages taken from their context.

While the Germans generally invoked more militant prophets than Fichte to lead them during the War, Fichte was a welcome target for the Allies. In France, Goblot opened fire with " L'origine de la folie allemande. Les Discours à la Nation Allemande de Fichte." [54] Goblot dealt only with the *Reden*, which he considered the " philosophic basis for German madness," Pan-Germanism, and other evils. IIe mentioned the fact that a new French translation of the *Reden* appeared during the War. At the same time he indicated that the *Reden* had to be misinterpreted to become a source of evil.

A similar article was that of Declareuil, " Les Discours à la Nation Allemande de J. G. Fichte." [55] It was very warlike in spirit and made Fichte the father of Pan-Germanism and of the worst elements in German nationalism. It pointed out that new editions of the *Reden* had appeared at very important dates in German history,[56] and the *Reden* were styled the *bréviaire de nationalisme germain*.

In Italy Felice Momigliano took up the cudgels against Fichte in an article entitled " Amadeo Fichte e le caratteristiche del nazionalismo tedesco." [57] He placed the *Reden* in the foreground and maintained that the cosmopolite Fichte had been converted to nationalism. He also mentioned the significant fact that the *Reden* had been translated into Italian for the first time during the World War.

[54] *Revue du Mois*, 1915, pp. 687-708.

[55] *Revue du Droit et de la Science Politique*, vol. 34 (1917), pp. 361-403.

[56] Editions of the *Reden* in German appeared in 1808, 1824, 1859, 1868/69, 1871, 1896, 1908, 1909, 1912, 1919, and no doubt there were others.

[57] *Nuova Antologia*, vol. 185 (1916), pp. 62-75.

In the English-speaking world the work of Santayana, John Dewey, and J. Holland Rose appeared, and on a much lower scale, that of Legge. Santayana and Rose protested that their work was not the product of the war, and they were quite right. Their view of Fichte was well established in the historiography of all countries.[58]

Thus the World War brought to natural fruition the seed that had been sown for more than a half-century. A German national hero and prophet naturally became a " villain " to the Allies.

When the War was over, the Germans found themselves in dire distress. The war had gone against them and they had been compelled to sign a treaty that placed heavy burdens upon them for an indefinite period. Starvation stalked through the land and revolution was just around the corner. The French invasion of the Ruhr roused the entire country to patriotic fury and the disastrous collapse of the mark caused untold hardships. The skies were black with impending ruin and deep pessimism and despair took hold of the nation. It was Germany's dark hour.

German leaders felt that the spirit of the people must be roused and that they must be led out of their slough of despond. What better for the purpose than a strong dose of Fichte? Here was a man who believed in the Germans and in their destiny and who had said some wonderful things about them. Hence his was good medicine for despairing patriots.

The result was what Johnsen calls a " Fichte Renaissance." [59] The movement was undoubtedly spontaneous, but its widespread character was astounding. Newspapers and journals commented on Fichte, addresses were deliv-

---

[58] The estimates of Santayana, Dewey, and Rose have been treated in the Introduction. See pp. 9-12.

[59] *Op. cit.*, Introduction.

ered, a *Deutscher Fichte Bund* was organized under eminent auspices, universities in all parts of the country assigned Fichte for *Dr. phil.* dissertations, and many new Fichte books appeared on the market. The *Reden* were again reprinted (1919). Thus the Fichte Renaissance was in full swing.

The general character of the new Fichtean literature was patriotic and not scholarly. The half-dozen *Dr. phil.* theses, for instance, which were accessible for examination, are strongly patriotic in spirit, but second-rate products of scholarship. They omit many of the important works of Fichte, they show no acquaintance with the important secondary works, and they again place the *Reden* in the foreground and make them unique in Fichte's writings. For the most part they are patriotic tracts, and this is frequently indicated in their titles. No purpose is served in citing this literature in detail. A few examples will suffice.[60]

Karl Haack wrote his *Der religieuse und ethische Charakter der Vaterlandsliebe Fichtes* in 1927. In his Introduction he declares that in Fichte's day the problem of Germany was nationalism versus cosmopolitanism; today it is nationalism versus internationalism. Fichte will be helpful in routing the sinister forces of internationalism.[61] Helmuth Johnsen's thesis (Erlangen, 1929),[62] a much better piece of work, in spite of its criticism of "political propaganda" in Fichtean literature, portrays a highly patriotic Fichte and omits the leading secondary works in its bibliography. *Der Deutsche Fichte Bund,* apparently a develop-

---

[60] A good deal of this literature may be found in the bibliographies of Karl Haack, *Der religieuse und ethische Charakter der Vaterlandsliebe Fichtes,* and Konrad Reidt, *Das Nationale und das Übernationale bei Fichte unter besonderer Berücksichtigung seiner Pädagogik.*

[61] *Op. cit.,* p. 9.

[62] *Das Staatsideal J. G. Fichtes.*

ment of the *Fichte Gesellschaft von 1914*, gives as its purpose " the propagation and development of that national strength and unity which was revealed at the outbreak of the War." [63]

In this connection it is interesting to note that Ebert's speech at the opening of the National Assembly at Weimar in February, 1919, included the following:

In this way we will set to work, our great aim ever before us: to maintain the rights of the German nation, to lay the foundations in Germany for a strong democracy, and to achieve this in the true social spirit and in the socialistic way. Thus shall we realize that which Fichte has given to the German nation as its task. We will establish a state of justice and truthfulness, founded on the equality of all humanity.[64]

But the Fichtean Renaissance is not made up of such material entirely. The scholarly and critical historiography of pre-war times has also survived and produced some excellent works. Certain outstanding examples of this may find space here.

In 1920 Gustav Kafka undertook to psychoanalyze Fichte on the basis of his letters and writings. His study, " Erlebnis und Theorie in Fichtes Lehre vom Verhältnis der Geschlechter. Eine charakterologische Studie," [65] is based chiefly on Fichte's letters to his wife, his lowly origin, and his insistence that a man's philosophy is a reflection of his personality. He concludes that Fichte suffered badly from a sense of inferiority and repression which found an outlet in his great emphasis on the importance of the personal

[63] " Will die völkische Kraft und Einmütigkeit, wie sie sich zu Kriegsbeginn offenbarte, wachhalten und fördern." See inside cover of pamphlet *Fichte unser Führer* (Hamburg, no date).

[64] English translation of the *Addresses* (Open Court, Chicago and London, 1922), Introduction, p. xxii.

[65] *Zeitschrift für Angewandte Psychologie*, vol. 16 (1920), pp. 1-24.

Ego. The study is important also for the reason that it calls attention to the general lack of esteem in which Fichte was held during his lifetime and to the repeated accusations of megalomania against him.

The decade after the War also produced some important new source material on Fichte. Hans Schulz published a new and highly desirable collection of Fichte's correspondence.[66] The old edition compiled by Fichte's son had become inadequate because of new finds. Further material was added in Runze's *Neue Fichte Funde aus der Heimat und Schweiz* (1919), which dealt chiefly with Fichte's early life. In 1923 Wilhelm Flitner published the inaccessible Masonic lectures, *Philosophie der Maurerei (Briefe an Konstant)*, which were not included in either the I. H. Fichte or the Medicus edition of the Works, and prefaced them with an excellent Introduction.

At the same time separate volumes were published which contained Fichte's neglected political works. The best of these are Otto Braun, *Johann Gottlieb Fichte, Volk und Staat. Eine Auswahl aus seinen Schriften* (1921), and Reinhold Strecker, *Fichtes Politische Fragmente* (1925). Mention should also be made of the excellent critical article by Wilhelm Erben, " Fichte Studien." [67] Erben points out the unscholarly editing of I. H. Fichte and adds important notes on Fichte's language.

Important secondary works also appeared during this decade, such as those of Gertrud Bäumer, Nico Wallner, and Max Wundt.[68] But the outstanding contribution is perhaps that of Rudolf Körner, " Die Wirkungen der

[66] Hans Schulz, *Fichtes Briefwechsel*, 2 vols.

[67] *Historische Vierteljahrschrift*, vol. 21 (1922/23), pp. 282-304.

[68] Gertrud Bäumer, *Fichte und sein Werk* (1921) ; Nico Wallner, *Fichte als politischer Denker* (1926) ; Max Wundt, *Fichte Forschungen* (1929).

Reden Fichtes " (1927).[69]　Körner documents the suggestions offered earlier by Jürgen Bona Meyer and assails the
entire national legend which surrounds the *Reden*.　There
has been a rather significant silence in regard to this study.
It is not noticed in any bibliography nor has anyone deigned
to reply to it.

Outside of Germany the Fichtean Renaissance produced
important results, some of which must be noted here.　The
greatest single study on Fichte has been published in
France—*Fichte et son temps*, by Xavier Léon.　Léon's first
volume on Fichte, devoted almost entirely to metaphysics,
was published in 1902.　*Fichte et son temps* was in preparation for thirteen years; it was in the hands of the publisher
in 1914.　The War prevented its publication until 1922-27.
Léon has not only added a vast amount of new material
to Fichtean studies, but his interpretation is a challenge.
From start to finish Fichte remains to Léon a republican
with socialist leanings.　All else is secondary, even his
nationalism.

In 1927 appeared another remarkable French book.　Victor Basch, professor at the Sorbonne, champion of international conciliation and prominent member of the League
for the Rights of Man, published a small volume entitled
*Les doctrines politiques des philosophes classiques de l'Alle-
magne*.　Basch had embraced German Idealism with great
enthusiasm.　But during the War, German Idealism was
accused of being one of the chief causes of the catastrophe.
Basch's book is a re-examination of the political doctrines
of the classic German Idealists, Leibnitz, Kant, Fichte, and
Hegel.　Basch undertakes an exoneration of the Idealists

---

[69] *Forschungen zur Brandenburgisch und Preussischen Geschichte,* vol.
40, pt. 1 (1927), pp. 65-87.

and re-affirms his faith in them.[70]   Right or wrong, Basch's little volume has its importance in Fichtean historiography.

The Italian, Giuseppe Maggiore, reverts to Fichte twice after the War, once to compare him to Gioberti (1919) and the second time to save him for socialism.   His *Fichte, Studio critico sul fiosofo del nazionalismo socialista* (1921) points out what happened to Fichte during the War and goes on to emphasize his national socialism.

After Fascism captured the state in Italy, its political theorists began to wage war on Liberalism, Democracy, and Socialism, and their philosophical bases.   According to an address delivered by Signor Rocco at Perugia in 1925,[71] which received the enthusiastic endorsement of Mussolini, Fascism is opposed to these three.   Rocco goes further. He endeavors to clear the good name of Italy from any charge of ever having trafficked with liberalism.   He concedes that Marsilius of Padua was Italian, but he wrote for a German, Ludwig the Bavarian.   After that, all the liberal theorists are non-Italian—English, French, Scottish, Dutch, or German.   Among the Germans, Fichte is specifically mentioned.

Two more notes may find a place here for the light they shed on recent interpretations of Fichte.   Among the novels dealing with the War and its suffering is *Siberian Garrison* by the Hungarian, Rodion Markovits,[72] an excellent description of prison life in Siberia.   When the Austrian and Hungarian soldiers sought diversion for their weary days in prison camp, they arranged for study classes on various

[70] See Preface, pp. vi-ix; for significant comment on Basch's general conclusions see the review by Carlton J. H. Hayes in the *American Historical Review*, July, 1928.

[71] Milford W. Howard, *Fascism a Challenge to Democracy*, pp. 56-70; also *International Conciliation* (1925).

[72] English translation (New York, Liveright, 1929).

subjects taught by the university men among the prisoners. A class in socialism was organized and in this Fichte was studied together with Saint-Simon, Robert Owen, Marx, and Lassalle.

Finally, a note on the USSR. Traveling in that country in 1929, the present writer visited the Marx-Engels Institute in Moscow and had a lengthy discussion with the Director. The Marx-Engels Institute devotes its energies to the study of Marx, Engels, the labor movement, the Internationals, and the revolutionary movement in all countries. Its libraries are arranged according to countries. In the German section Fichte was well represented. The Director declared that a letter from Xavier Léon, the French Fichtean authority, was on file which stated that in his opinion the Marx-Engels Institute had the best collection of Fichteana in the world. The Director was proud of this collection, because " Fichte was one of the greatest German revolutionaries."

Thus the cycle is again complete. During his lifetime Fichte was a Jacobin and revolutionary to his contemporaries and remained such for the Prussian reactionaries even in the 1820's. After 1840, and especially after 1862, he was thought of chiefly as a nationalist and patriot, though the socialists and liberals did not forget him. And now, after the World War, we again find all shades of interpretation represented — extreme nationalism to revolutionary bolshevism.

APPENDIX

Fichte and Freemasonry

Fichte's membership in Freemasonry was frequently cited against him. The following notes on French Freemasonry—a subject urgently in need of further exploration—will explain the attitude of his contemporaries. " Brother Fichte's " relationship to the order furnishes an interesting sidelight on his life and thought.

If we accept 1717 as the birth year of modern speculative Freemasonry and England as the country of its birth,[1] we must note that in 1721 a French lodge was founded at Dunkirk and by 1725 there was a lodge in Paris. The number of lodges increased rapidly in France in spite of varied opposition. By 1756 there were 300 lodges and at the outbreak of the Revolution there were 629.[2] In 1737 the police forbade membership in the order and tried to suppress it, but without success. In 1738 the first of a long series of papal

---

[1] Whatever the antiquity of certain elements of Masonic ritual, it is difficult to prove that the essential attributes of the institution now known as Freemasonry antedate the eighteenth century. Most historians are satisfied to date the modern speculative movement from the famous meeting of 1717. See Em. Rebold, *Histoire des trois grandes loges de Franc-Maçons en France* (Paris, 1864) ; Heinrich Boos, *Geschichte der Freimaurerei* (Aarau, 1906), p. 169.

[2] Wilhelm Ohr, *Der französische Geist und die Freimaurerei* (Leipzig, 1916). This is a war book and hostile to the Grand Orient and to France, but it is useful for its frequent and abundant citations from Masonic sources.

condemnations appeared,[3] the bull *In eminenti*. Still the
" English poison " continued to spread.

Eighteenth-century France was an attractive place for a
group whose platform included the equality of all men.[4]
Freemasonry speedily became in France an important rally-
ing point for egalitarians. The philosophy of the *Aufklärung* was eagerly absorbed within the lodges. French Freemasonry became anti-monarchic and anti-clerical.

Its egalitarian philosophy was well expressed by one of
its Grand Masters, the Duke of Autin, in 1740:

> Men are not essentially divided by the difference in the languages
> they speak, the clothes they wear, the countries they inhabit, or
> the dignities with which they are clothed. The whole world is
> really one great republic, every nation in it is a family, every
> individual a child. To give new life to these fundamental prin-
> ciples and to spread them, since they are taken from human
> nature itself, for that purpose primarily was our society
> founded.[5]

In 1738 Ramsay suggested to the French Masons that
they publish an encyclopaedia in which this new universal
knowledge should be contained. The idea was received with
enthusiasm, and Diderot, a Mason, became editor of the project. The first volume of the famous *Encyclopaedia*
appeared in 1752.[6]

At this time the French lodges adopted as their motto the
words *Liberté, Egalité,* and *Fraternité.* There was in this

[3] Others followed in the years 1751, 1814, 1821, 1825, 1829, 1832, 1846,
1849, 1854, 1864, 1865, 1873, 1884, etc. See Boos, *op. cit.,* p. 181.

[4] Louis Gottschalk, *The Era of the French Revolution* (New York,
1929), p. 82.

[5] Ohr, *op. cit.,* pp. 30-31; also Lennhoff, *Die Freimaurerei* (Zurich,
1929), pp. 82-110: " Die französische Maurerei."

[6] Lennhoff, *op. cit.,* p. 89.

period also a conflict within the order between the nobility and the ever-increasing bourgeois membership concerning the symbols and practices which the nobles had imported from chivalry. The bourgeois opposed this innovation and wished to retain the more democratic symbols of the builders.

After 1771 the republican members of the order became very active. They proposed to organize all lodges on a democratic basis and to stand openly against all inequalities. There was some opposition to this plan, hence this group separated from the Grande Loge Nationale and carried most lodges with themselves into secession. This new and dominant group called itself the Grand Orient (1773).

Among the members of French Freemasonry were many of the later leaders of the Revolution, such as Sieyès, Marat, Condorcet, Mirabeau, Barnave, Pétion, Boissy d'Anglas, Dupont de Nemours, Robespierre, the Abbé Grégoire, Diderot, Helvetius, Camille Desmouslins, Danton, Brissot, and others.[7]

Besides spreading the ideas of rationalism, the Freemasons of France frequently undertook to challenge and correct the evils of their day in accordance with their principles. They were actively engaged in the reform of justice. In the Calas case Voltaire's protest was followed by Elie de Beaumont's representation of the case before the courts. Both were Masons. In 1785 three peasants were condemned to death for petty thievery. The Freemasons undertook to save their lives. One of their group, Dupaty, waged an active campaign for the condemned, the lodges openly espoused their cause, and the peasants were freed.[8]

From all this it is clear that the French lodges were differ-

[7] Lennhoff, *op. cit.*, p. 94.
[8] Lennhoff, *op. cit.*, p. 98.

ent in character from the social and philanthropic lodges of the Scottish rite. By their espousal of Rousseau and Voltaire, their opposition to irresponsible monarchy, clericalism, injustice, and privilege, and by their attempt to reform the morals of the age, they prepared the way for the Revolution.

When the Revolution came, the Freemasons were at first among the leaders. Many of the most articulate *cahiers* were written by Freemasons.[9] But after a short time the situation changed, and the order was suppressed. The reason for this is probably to be found in its profession and practice of cosmopolitanism and egalitarianism. In the army, for instance, there were 73 regimental lodges in 1787. The idea of equality ruled and many a subaltern was the Masonic superior of his military commander. This undermined discipline and made the army inefficient. Further, the idea of fraternity bridged national frontiers even in the army. The distress signal would prevent one Mason from firing on another, it prevented the capture of an enemy prize on the seas, and caused many other utterly unmilitary acts.[10] This fraternization was dangerous and was recognized as such. Suppression resulted. The order was revived again in 1800 under Napoleon and carried on its work as previously.[11]

Freemasons have frequently claimed credit for the Revolution. Thus Felix Portal:

In the lodges the means were studied by which to remedy the decay from which the society of the *ancien régime* suffered. In the lodges the Encyclopaedia was prepared, that miracle book from which the revolutionary spirit of the eighteenth century

[9] Gottschalk, *op. cit.*, p. 118.

[10] H. Soanen, "La Franc-Maçonnerie et l'armée pendant la Révolution et l'Empire," *Annales Historiques de la Révolution Française*, vol. 5 (1928), pp. 530-540.

[11] A. Mathiez, "La Franc-Maçonnerie en l'an VII et en l'an IX," *Révolution Française*, vol. 40 (1901), pp. 30-35.

derived. From the work of the lodges the French Revolution took its beginning.

And again Bernardin:

The Word of Freemasonry was made flesh [in the French Revolution]. Freemasonry gave to the world the Declaration of the Rights of Man and Citizen and to France the Constitution of 1791. In this way it embodied its doctrines in a new social and political organization.

A pronunciamento of the Grand Orient at the close of the nineteenth century declared:

It was Freemasonry which prepared the way for our Revolution, the greatest of all heroic epics of the people known to the annals of history; and to Freemasonry belongs the honor of giving to this unforgettable event the formula in which its principles were embodied.[2]

Further evidence for the revolutionary character of the Grand Orient may be found in the attacks of its enemies, particularly in two outstanding works of the time. One was by an Englishman, Robison, who in his *Proofs of a Conspiracy* (1797) expressed his astonishment and fear concerning Freemasonry on the continent, and especially in France. Robison was himself an English Mason, author, scientist, contributor to the *Encyclopaedia Britannica*. He traveled a great deal, in France, Germany, and Russia, and was astonished to find the lodges on the continent enthusiastic adherents of the new social philosophy. His book is the work of a man frightened to the point of panic by the " conspiracy " he had observed.

The other is the work of the Abbé Barruel, *Mémoires pour servir à l'histoire du Jacobinisme*. The Abbé hated the

[12] For these citations see Ohr, *op. cit.*, pp. 34, 35, 196-203.

Jacobins and all revolutionaries as destroyers of religion, government, and the rights of property. In five bulky volumes he "exposed" the intrigues of the secret Illuminati who operated through the Jacobins and the Freemasons. In volume V he paid his respects to Fichte:

In Saxony, for example, at Jena, a professor is permitted to instruct youth, telling them that governments are contrary to the laws of Reason and Humanity, and that therefore in twenty, in fifteen, perhaps even in ten years there will be no further government in the world.[8]

Fichte's relation to Freemasonry, then, must be understood against this background: the revolutionary character of the Grand Orient. Let us now proceed to Fichte's participation in the work of the Masonic lodge.

Fichte always emphasized the power of education. In social life (*Geselligkeit*) employed for intelligent conversation he saw an educative factor. He declared that "discussion with men and women who do not reason academically is of enormous value and would be the greatest aid to academic teachers and professors who practice it least."[14] For the same reasons he looked with favor upon all manner of societies which had a serious purpose. He encouraged such societies at Jena, particularly the *Bund der freien Männer*. Since his age was one of great intellectual ferment, the discussions under Fichte's leadership were anything but dull.

Considerations such as these were in Fichte's mind when he joined the Freemasons in 1793. At first he hesitated, because he was under the impression that the order offered purely social advantages, but soon he convinced himself that he had been mistaken. His correspondence with Theodor

---

[13] *Op. cit.*, vol. v, pp. 229, 230, 244, 245; also cited in Léon, *op. cit.*, vol. ii, p. 20.

[14] Flitner, *Philosophie der Maurerei* (Leipzig, 1923), p. vii.

von Schoen in 1792 illuminates the whole situation. Asked whether he is a Mason, Fichte had then replied:

1 am not a Mason. Despite the many reasons which might induce me to join, I have more important reasons to remain out of the order. I am—pardon me if you are already initiated— as thoroughly convinced as an uninitiated may be that the order has no universal purpose, rather that its whole task is to search for such a purpose which it hopes to discover in symbols and ancient rites. I further believe that many another society has taken refuge behind the order in order to achieve its particular purpose under the guise of Freemasonry.

Nevertheless he planned to join the order " for higher purposes."

For it seems to me that our times, reduced to slavery by its luxuries and subject to all corruption, has bitter need of a society which would be for it a source of all that is good, which might become for it approximately what the *Vehmgericht* and knighthood were for our corrupt ancestors. For this, Freemasonry might qualify, not in its present constitution, but at least in its present accepted form.—I should like to help achieve something of that kind—but I speak now of mere dreams and only to a friend such as you. Go ahead and join the lodge. God willing we shall meet some day.[15]

This letter foreshadows Fichte's purpose, if and when he should decide to join the order. When he was in Zurich in 1793 he became a Freemason. He wrote to von Schoen:

I have many plans, ideas, and hopes in regard to my membership for which I need the aid of men of good will.[16]

When Fichte arrived at Jena there was no Masonic lodge

[15] See Hans Schulz, *Fichtes Briefwechsel*, vol. i, pp. 251, 257 *et seq.*; also Flitner, *op. cit.*, pp. x, xi.

[16] Hans Schulz, *op. cit.*, vol. i, p. 301.

in that city—not since 1764. For that reason he joined the lodge *Günther zum stehenden Löwen* in Rudolstadt. In 1799, when Fichte became involved in the charge of atheism, he quite naturally sought support from the Masons and especially from the head of his lodge, upon whom there would seem to rest an obligation to render assistance to a victim of religious intolerance. But the lodge and its leader failed him completely and Fichte left for Berlin.

In Berlin the Lodge of the " Royal York for Friendship " had been established under Frederick the Great. It had been founded in 1752 by French scholars and artists whom the Prussian king had invited to Berlin.[17] This lodge was affiliated with the Grand Orient of France. For more than twenty-five years it had carried on its business in French, since its members were chiefly Frenchmen. After 1778, however, Germans began to invade the lodge and with them the German language. This change in membership was also the occasion for various other changes.[18]

When Fichte arrived at Berlin he made contacts with lodge members almost immediately, such as the writer Rhode and the merchant Basset. They were so astonished at his knowledge of Freemasonry that they called the attention of the Grand Master, Ignaz Fessler, to the newcomer. Fessler had come to Freemasonry through a study of Kant, whose ideas he was determined to spread in the lodge. When Fessler met Fichte he was at once impressed with the latter's thorough acquaintance with Masonic lore. He determined to get his aid in his own plans for the reorganization of the Berlin lodge. For a time he was evidently much taken by Fichte's personality. He wrote concerning him:

[17] Léon, *op. cit.*, vol. ii, pp. 1-57, where also an unusual bibliography will be found in the footnotes.

[18] Léon, " Fessler, Fichte, et la Loge Royale York à Berlin," *Revue de Métaphysique et de Morale*, vol. xvi (1908), pp. 813-843.

His [Fichte's] personal behavior has already changed many an opponent of his philosophical system into a friend of the man in him.[19]

But while Fessler planned to use Fichte for his purposes, Fichte hoped to make Fessler his tool for his own projects. He wrote to his wife:

I have got next to his tricks. Discretion is necessary in dealing with a man who has not the slightest notion as to who I am and what my purposes are and whom I shall have to make use of in the end.[20]

What both men had in mind was a reformation and reorganization of the lodge. When the increasing German membership and the use of the German language made necessary a revision of the constitution and ritual of the Berlin lodge, Fessler, in 1796, had been won over to undertake the task. Fessler did revise the ritual in 1797 and was busily engaged in revising the constitution when Fichte made his appearance. Fessler's purpose was to make of the lodge an agency for the rule of Reason over man's sensuous nature. For this he desired Fichte's assistance, yet he did not wish a " professional scholar " to overshadow him in his task. He was apparently intensely jealous of Fichte's influence over against his own. Fichte, on the other hand, had somewhat different goals in mind, which he frequently discussed with Varnhagen von Ense. Varnhagen has summarized Fichte's ideas in his *Denkwürdigkeiten*:

To make of this order of brothers with its branches throughout the world an effective agent of Philosophy, to order its degrees according to the light of Science, and thus to create in our day

---

[19] Hans Schulz, "Aus Fichtes Leben," *Kantstudien*, Ergänzungsheft, no. 44 (1918), p. 29.

[20] Flitner, *op. cit.*, p. xii.

a sort of Pythagorean institute: such a plan had in it something extremely attractive for a man like Fichte, who saw in it great promise for the future.[21]

On April 11, 1800 Fichte was received into the Berlin lodge. On April 13 and 27 he delivered his Masonic lectures before large audiences. They appeared later in garbled form and with many additions as *Briefe an Konstant.*[22] Fichte advanced rapidly in the various degrees, and as early as May 8, 1800 he received the eighth and highest degree, the Inner Orient. He was also elected Grand Orator with the duty of addressing the lodge every second Sunday.

Meanwhile trouble was brewing for the lodge from another quarter. In 1798 the king of Prussia had suppressed all secret societies. Several lodges had managed to escape the ban, among them the Royal York. This caused much jealousy among the members of the suppressed societies. Royal York was attacked from many quarters, partly because it was adopting Kantian ideas under Fessler's leadership. It was called a secret Jacobin club. The Abbé Barruel thought it a very suspicious feature that the lodge imitated the French governmental organization by ordering its affairs through a Directory, a Senate of Ancients, and a Senate of Youth. These suspicions from without may explain the events that followed.

From the very outset, relations between Fessler and Fichte had been strained. They were jealous of one another and there was a complete lack of mutual trust. Each wished to use the other for his purposes and both were therefore disingenuous in their personal relations. This personal incompatibility soon expressed itself in open antagonism. In

[21] Varnhagen von Ense, *Denkwürdigkeiten und Vermischte Schriften.* vol. i, p. 290.

[22] See page 72.

an address to the lodge brothers, Fichte made an attack on the *Euergeten,* a secret society which had been suppressed by royal decree. But Fessler had been a founder of this group. In a letter to the king the group tried to defend themselves against the accusation of Jacobinism by the fact that Fessler had reorganized the Freemasons along the lines of the *Euergeten* and the Freemasons were permitted to continue unmolested. Fichte's attack led to Fessler's counter-attack and further charges by Fichte. The whole matter led to an open scandal in the lodge, whereupon Fichte resigned on July 7, 1800 after a very brief membership.

This was probably the end of Fichte's active participation in the Masonic order, though he retained throughout his days a high regard for the work of Freemasonry. True, he declared in a letter to Fr. Schlegel on August 16, 1800:

Freemasonry has bored me to such an extent, and then made me so indignant, that I have taken final leave from it.[23]

None the less he permitted the publication of his addresses to the order in 1802/03, and in 1806 he wrote to his wife: "Dear precious Masonry, how it does help!"[24] Even in 1811 he expressed to Varnhagen von Ense a high opinion of Freemasonry as a school of noble humanity.[25]

Fichte's membership in Freemasonry and his purpose in the order thus fit very well into his life and thought. He saw in the order a possible tool for remaking society and regenerating mankind. Within the scheme of his philosophy this involved a wholly new political and cultural orientation for the order.[26] He failed in his effort, as did Fessler, who also left the order shortly after Fichte's departure. The

---

[23] Hans Schulz, *Aus Fichtes Leben*, p. 32.

[24] *Fichtes Leben*, vol. i, p. 369.

[25] Varnhagen von Ense, *op. cit.*, vol. ii, p. 328.

[26] It is interesting to note that Fr. Schlegel and F. Baader referred to

whole story is a significant episode which vividly illuminates Fichte's ethical activism. Meanwhile, Freemasonry has ever pointed with pride to " Brother Fichte " and continues to cite his lectures as a guiding star.[27]

Fichte's Masonic membership as evidence that Freemasonry was the source of his entire social and political philosophy. See Léon, *op. cit.*, vol. ii, p. 57.

[27] See, e. g. Lennhoff, *op. cit.*, index under " Fichte."

BIBLIOGRAPHY

SOURCES

Fichtes Werke, 8 vols., edited by I. H. Fichte, Berlin, Veit und Cie., 1845.

Fichtes Nachgelassene Werke, 3 vols., edited by I. H. Fichte, Bonn, Marcus, 1834.

Fichtes Werke, 6 vols., edited by Fritz Medicus, Leipzig, Meiner, 1911-12.

The standard edition of Fichte's Works is that edited by his son, Immanuel Hermann Fichte, in the 11 volumes cited. This is the oldest and most complete edition of Fichte's writings and all references in this study are made to it unless otherwise noted.

Serious criticism has recently appeared, indicating that Fichte's son was not a conscientious editor. He apparently conceived his task to be the publication of a text, the language of which was "modern" and unobjectionable to his *Sprachgefühl*. Accordingly he took considerable license with the original manuscript and "corrected" what appeared to him to be archaic or clumsy expressions. In the *Patriotic Dialogues* he even went so far as to eliminate the word "Prussian" before patriotism twice, thus removing a possible offense to ardent nationalists. The extent to which this "correction" was practiced has never been fully examined, but where the examination has been made, the editor's changes have been shown to be very considerable. Medicus, for example, requires 13 pages to list the "corrections" of one short work. (See Medicus edition, vol. vi, pp. 627-639.) Many others are indicated by Wilhelm Erben in a very suggestive study. (See "Fichte Studien" in *Historische Vierteljahrschrift*, vol. xxi (1922-23), pp. 282-304.) A study of Fichte's language is clearly impossible until an accurate text has been published. Fichte's great emphasis on language made him a meticulous stylist who not only revised with great care what he had written but also sought to improve his style by translations from other languages. No scientific study of Fichte's language has ever been made; certainly it is impossible to undertake the task with the present corrupt text. (See Max Wund, *Fichte Forschungen*: "Fichtes Sprache," pp. 372-374.)

Aside from language, the I. H. Fichte edition is not complete. Once the editor adds a very badly chosen title. The arrangement and order of the various works also shows bad judgment. (See Kuno Fischer, *Fichte*, pp. 323-333 for criticism and suggested re-arrangement.)

The Medicus edition is much better in arrangement and now and then in text. Medicus, for instance, restored the text of *Das System der Rechtslehre*, 1812, which Fichte's son had marred badly by his additions. He also removed the objectionable title from *Die Staatslehre*, 1813, using instead Fichte's own introductory words. Two important criticisms of it must be made. It is not based independently on Fichte's manuscripts, but merely reproduces the text of I. H. Fichte's edition. Essentially, therefore, it is likewise a corrupt and inaccurate text. Further, the edition is even less complete than I. H. Fichte's. Since most references to Fichte's Works are to the original I. H. Fichte edition, Medicus notes in the margin the volume and page of the original.

FURTHER SOURCE MATERIALS

Fichte, I. H., *Fichtes Leben und literarischer Briefwechsel*, 2 vols., 1st edition, Sulzbach, Brockhaus, 1830; 2nd enlarged edition 1862.

Schulz, Hans, *Fichtes Briefwechsel*, 2 vols., Jena, H. Haessel, 1925.

Schulz, Hans, *Aus Fichtes Leben. Briefe und Mitteilungen zu einer kuenftigen Sammlung von Fichtes Briefwechsel*, in *Kantstudien*, Ergaenzungshefte no. 44, 1918.

The edition of Fichte's letters by his son has been entirely superseded by Hans Schulz' collection of 1925, for which his study in the *Kantstudien* was preparatory. The Fichte biography by his son is basic to all others.

Fichte, J. G., *Philosophie der Maurerei* (*Briefe an Konstant*), edited by Wilhelm Flitner, Leipzig, Meiner, 1923.

These Masonic lectures appear in neither edition of the *Werke*. They have an exceedingly interesting literary and textual history, for which see p. 72.

Runze, Maximilian, *Neue Fichtefunde aus der Heimat und Schweiz*, Gotha, Perthes, 1919.

Schulz, Hans, *Johann Gottlieb Fichte als Hauslehrer*, *Paedagogisches Magazin*, no. 790, 1919, Langensalza, Beyer.

Contains Fichte's diary from August 2 to September 20, 1789.

Weinhold, M., *48 Briefe von J. G. Fichte und seinen Verwandten*, Leipzig, 1862.

From Fichte's early life.

TWO USEFUL COLLECTIONS OF IMPORTANT POLITICAL WRITINGS

Braun, Otto (ed.), *Johann Gottlieb Fichte, Volk und Staat. Eine Auswahl aus seinen Schriften* (in series *Der Deutsche Staatsgedanke*), Munich, Drei Masken Verlag, 1921.

Strecker, R. (ed.), *Fichtes Politische Fragmente*, Leipzig, Meiner, 1925.

Many works of Fichte have been reprinted in various editions and translations.

Secondary Works on Fichte

Adamson, R., *Fichte.* Edinburg and London, Blackwood, 1881.

Adler, Max, *Wegweiser. Studien zur Geistesgeschichte des Sozialismus.* Stuttgart, Dietz, 1914, pp. 78-108.

Ahlgrimm, Elisabeth, *Kultur und Staat bei Fichte.* Oesterwieck, am Harz, A. W. Zickfeldt, 1921.

Andler, Charles, *Nietzsche, sa vie et sa pensée,* vol. i: *Les precurseurs de Nietzsche.* Paris, Editions Bossard, 1920.

Anonymous, *Fichte und die deutsche Not. Zeitgemaesse Randbemerkungen von einem der Deutschland lieb hat.* Berlin, 1919.

Anonymous, " Fichtes Lehre von der aeusseren Politik." *Sueddeutsche Monatshefte.* Vol. 14 (1917), pp. 467-478.

Armstrong, A. C., " Fichte's conception of a league of nations," *Journal of Philosophy.* Vol. xxix, p. 6, Mar. 17, 1932, pp. 153-158.

Baeumer, Gertrud, *Fichte und sein Werk.* Berlin, Herbig, 1921.

Basch, Victor, *Les doctrines politiques des philosophes classiques de l'Allemagne.* Paris, F. Alcan, 1927.

Bauch, Bruno A. C., " Fichte und der deutsche Staatsgedanke," *Paedagogisches Magazin.* No. 1045, Langensalza, 1925.

Bergmann, Ernst, *Fichte als Erzieher zum Deutschtum.* Leipzig, Meiner, 1915.

Bernstein, Eduard, " Wie Fichte und Lassalle national waren." *Archiv fuer die Geschichte des Sozialismus und der Arbeiterbewegung.* vol. 5 (1914), pp. 143-162.

Binder, Julius, " Fichte und die Nation," *Logos.* Vol. 10 (1921-22), pp. 275-315.

Bluntschli, J. C., *Geschichte des Allgemeinen Staatsrechts und der Politik.* 1864, 2nd edition, 1867, Munich, Cotta.

Boos, Heinrich, *Geschichte der Freimaurerei. Ein Beitrag zur Kultur- und Literaturgeschichte des 18. Jahrhunderts.* 2nd edition, Aarau, Sauerlaender, 1906.

Busse, Wilhelm, *J. G. Fichte der Philosoph.* 2 vols., Halle, Heynemann, 1848-49.

Caspari, Otto, *Die Bedeutung des Freimaurertums fuer das geistige Leben.* 4th edition, Berlin, Unger, 1930.

Dawson, W. H., *The Evolution of Modern Germany.* London, Fisher Unwin, 1908.

Declareuil, J., " Les Discours à la Nation Allemand de J. Gottlieb Fichte," *Revue du Droit Public et de la Science Politique.* Vol. 34 (1917), pp. 361-403.

Dewey, John, *German Philosophy and Politics.* New York, Holt, 1915.

Diehl, Karl, *Deutschland als geschlossener Handelsstaat im Weltkriege.* Stuttgart, 1916.

Dosenheimer, Elise, "Fichtes Idee des deutschen Volkes." *Zeitschrift fuer Philosophie und Philosophische Kritik.* Vol. 156 (1915), pp. 11-28.

Dunning, W. A., *A history of political Theories from Rousseau to Spencer.* New York, MacMillan, 1920.

Eberhard, R., "Fichtes Gedanken über einen Völkerbund zur Aufrechterhaltung des Friedens." *Preussische Jahrbuecher,* 172 (June, 1918), pp. 394-401.

Encyclopaedia Britannica. 11th edition, "Fichte."

      Article by R. Adamson from earlier editions. Continued in later editions unsigned with additional bibliography.

Engel, Jakob, *Isokrates, Machiavelli, Fichte.* Magdeburg, E. Baensch, Jun., 1889.

Erben, Wilhelm, "Fichte Studien," *Historische Vierteljahrschrift.* Vol. xxi (1922/23), pp. 282-304.

Falckenberg, Richard, "J. G. Fichte. Ein Vortrag." *Zeitschrift füer Philosophie und Philosophische Kritik.* Vol. 156 (1915), pp. 3-11.

Fichte Gesellschaft, publications. Various dates and names.

Fischer, F., *Die Paedagogik Fichtes und Pestalozzis und die Gegenwart.* Greifswald, Emil Hartmann, 1926.

Fischer, Kuno, *Fichte* (in *Geschichte der neueren Philosophie,* vol. 5). Heidelberg, Bassermann, 1869.

Gelpcke, Ernest, *Fichte und die Gedankenwelt des Sturm und Drang.* Leipzig, Meiner, 1928.

Gladden, Washington, *Witnesses of the Light* (William Belden Noble Lectures for 1903). Boston and New York, Houghton Mifflin, 1903.

Gluecksohn, Moses, *Fichtes Staats und Wirtschaftslehre. Berner Studien zur Philosophie und ihrer Geschichte.* Vol. 70 (1910), Bern, Scheitlin & Cie.

Goblot, E., "L'origine philosophique de la folie allemande. Les Discours à la Nation Allemande de Fichte." *Revue du Mois* (1915), pp. 687-708.

Gottschalk, Louis, *The Era of the French Revolution.* New York, Houghton Mifflin, 1929.

La Grande Encyclopédie: "Franc-Maçonnerie" (unsigned).

Grau, Leonhard, *Die Voraussetzungen der Reden an die deutsche Nation von J. G. Fichte innerhalb seines Systems.* Homberg, Wiegand, 1900.

Gutman, S. Hirsch, *J. G. Fichtes Sozialpaedagogik.* Berner Studien zur Philosophie und ihrer Geschichte. Vol. 51 (1907), Bern, Sheitlin, Spring & Cie.

Haack, Karl, *Der religiöse und ethische Charakter der Vaterlandsliebe Fichtes.* Wohlau, Verlag "Schlesische Dorfzeitung," 1927.

Harms, Friedrich, *Rede zur Feier des hundertjährigen Geburtstages von Johann Gottlieb Fichte an der Christian-Albrechts Universität, gehalten am 19. Mai 1862.*

Hashagen, Justus, "Fichte und der Sozialismus." *Jahrbücher fuer Nationalökonomie und Statistik.* Vol. 136 (1932), pp. 495-498.

Heimsoeth, Heinz, *Fichte.* In series *Geschichte der Philosophie in Einzeldarstellungen.* Abt. VII, Bd. 29, Munich, 1923.

Hobohm, Mart., *Gedankenwelt Fichtes.* Burschenschaftliche Bücherei. vol. 2, Berlin, Boettger, 1904, pp. 347-396.

Jacoby, D., "Fichte und sein Verhaeltnis zu Preussen." *Euphorion.* Vol. 21 (1914), pp. 237-251.

Janson, Friedrich, *Fichtes Reden an die deutsche Nation. Eine Untersuchung ihres aktuell politischen Gehalts.* Abhandlungen zur Mittleren und Neuren Geschichte. No. 33, Berlin und Leipzig, 1911.

Janson, Friedrich, *Fichtes Reformplaene in den "Reden an die deutsche Nation" und ihr Zusammenhang mit den praktischen Reformen nach 1806.* Berlin und Leipzig, Rothschild, 1911.

Jobst, "Fichte und der Pazifismus." *Zeitschrift fuer Völkerfriede.* Vol. 18, 1918.

Jodl, "J. G. Fichte als Sozialpolitiker," *Zeitschrift fuer Philosophie und Philosophische Kritik.* N. s. vol. 112/3 (1898), pp. 191-216.

Johnsen, Helmuth, *Das Staatsideal J. G. Fichtes. Ein Beitrag zur Geschichte des deutschen Staatsgedankens.* Neustadt b. Coburg, Emil Patzschke, 1929.

Juvanon, Adrien, *Vers la Lumière. Quelques Pages d'Histoire Maçonnique.* Paris, Imprimerie Centrale de la Bourse, 1926.

Kafka, G., "Erlebnis und Theorie in Fichtes Lehre vom Verhältnis der Geschlechter. Eine charakterologische Studie," in *Zeitschrift für Angewandte Psychologie.* Vol. xvi (1920), pp. 1-24.

   A psycho-analytic study of Fichte's personality and its relation to his thought.

Koerner, Rud., "Die Wirkungen der Reden Fichtes," in *Forschungen zur Brandenburgisch und Preussischen Geschichte.* Vol. xl, pt. 1 (1927), pp. 65-87.

Lantoine, Albert, *Hiram Couronné d'Épines.* 2 vols., Paris, E. Nourry, 1926.

Lassalle, Ferdinand, *Die Philosophie Fichtes und die Bedeutung des deutschen Volksgeistes. Festrede am 19. Mai 1862.* 2d edition. Leipzig, J. Roetling, 1873.

Lassalle, Ferdinand, *Fichtes politisches Vermaechtnis und die neueste Gegenwart,* in Demokratische Studien, Hamburg, 1860.

Lassalle, Ferdinand, *Herr Julian Schmidt der Literarhistoriker mit Setzer-Scholien herausgegeben.* Berlin, G. Jansen, 1862.

Legge, J. G., *Rhyme and Revolution in Germany*. New York, Brentano, 1919.

Lehmann, Max, " Fichtes Reden an die deutsche Nation vor der preussischen Zensur." *Preussische Jahrbuecher*. Vol. 82 (1895), pp. 501-515.

Leibholz, Gerhard, *Fichte und der demokratische Gedanke*. Freiburg, no date.

Lennhoff, Eugen, *Die Freimaurerei*. Zuerich-Leipzig-Wien, Amalthea Verlag, 1929.

Léon, Xavier, " Fessler, Fichte, et la loge Royale York a Berlin," *Revue de Metaphysique et de Morale*. Vol. 16 (1908), pp. 813-843.

Léon, Xavier, *Fichte et son temps*. 2 vols. in 3, Paris, Colin, 1922-1927.

Léon's *Fichte et son temps* is easily the best work on Fichte, both factually and in interpretation. It was complete in 1913 and in the press in 1914. Léon had spent thirteen years writing it. It was brought to date before final publication in 1922-1927. Léon had access to many unpublished documents and discovered much new pertinent material.

Léon, Xavier, " La philosophie de Fichte," *Revue de Metaphysique et de Morale*. Vol. 10 (1902), pp. 26-68.

Léon, Xavier, *La Philosophie de Fichte*. *Ses rapports avec la conscience contemporaine*, Paris, Felix Alcan, 1902.

Lenoir, Raymond, " La doctrine de Fichte." *Revue Germanique*. Vol. xxii, 2, April-Jun, 1931, pp. 141-154.

Lindau, Hans, *Die Schriften zu J. G. Fichtes Atheismusstreit*. Munich, George Mueller, 1912.

Lindau, Hans, *Johann Gottlieb Fichtes Lehre von Staat und Gesellschaft in ihrem Verhältnis zum neueren Sozialismus*. Berlin, no publisher, 1899.

Maggiore, Giuseppe, *Fichte, Studio critico sul filosofo del nazionalismo socialista*. Citta di Castello, " Il Solco," 1921.

Maggiore, Guiseppe, *Gioberti e Fichte*. In " Pagine dell'ora." Milano, Fratelli Treves, 1919.

Markham, S. F., *A History of Socialism*. New York, Macmillan, 1931.

Martius, Goetz, *Johann Gottlieb Fichte*. Rede zur Feier des Geburtstages Seiner Majestaet des Deutschen Kaisers, Koenigs von Preussen Wilhelm II, gehalten an der Christian-Albrechts Universitaet am 27 Januar 1909. Kiel, Lipsius, 1909.

Mathiez, A., " La Franc-Maçonnerie en l'an VII et en l'an IX," *Révolution Française*. Vol. 40 (1901), pp. 30-35.

Mayer, Otto, *Fichte über das Volk*. Leipzig, Edelmann, 1913.

Medicus, Fritz, " J. G. Fichte als Anhänger und als Kritiker des Völkerbundgedankens," *Zeitschrift für Völkerrecht*. Vol. xi (1918), pp. 141-154.

Medicus, Fritz, *J. G. Fichte. Dreizehn Vorlesungen.* Berlin, Reuther und Reichardt, 1905.

Meinecke, Friedrich, *Fichte als nationaler Prophet.* Historisch und Politische Aufsätze, 1918.

Messer, A., "Fichte und Machiavelli," *Kantstudien.* 1920.

Meyer, Jürgen Bona, *Fichte, Lassalle und der Sozialismus.* Berlin, Carl Habel, 1878.

Meyer, Jürgen Bona, *Über Fichtes Reden an die deutsche Nation.* Hamburg, 1862.

Momigliano, Felice, "Amedeo Fichte e le caratteristiche del nazionalismo tedesco," *Nuova Antologia.* Vol. 185 (1916), pp. 62-75.

Noack, Ludwig, *Johann Gottlieb Fichte nach seinem Leben, Lehren und Wirken.* Leipzig, Wigand, 1862.

Oberdorfer, Aldo, "Machiavelli nel pensiero politico di J. G. Fichte," *Rivista d'Italia.* Vol. 19 (1916), pp. 285-332.

Ohr, Wilhelm, *Der französische Geist und die Freimaurerei.* Leipzig, Kochler, 1916.

Perego, Luigi, *L'idealismo etico di Fichte e il socialismo contemporaneo. Per una religione socialista.* Modena, A. F. Formiggini, 1911.

Petrone, Igino, *Lo stato mercantile chiuso di G. Am. Fichte e le premessa teorica del comunismo giuridico,* in *Atti della R. Accademia di Scienze Morali e Politiche.* Napoli, vol. 35-36 (1905-06), pp. 391-441.

Rebold, Em., *Histoire des trois grandes loges de Franc-Maçons en France.* Paris, Collignon, 1864.

Reichlin-Meldegg, K. A. von, "Der hundertste Geburtstag Johann Gottlieb Fichtes. Eine übersichtliche Darstellung der Fichtefestschriften," *Zeitschrift für Philosophie und Philosophische Kritik.* Vol. 42 (1863), pp. 242-277.

Reidt, Konrad, *Das Nationale und das Übernationale bei Fichte mit besonderer Berücksichtigung seiner Pädagogik.* Giessen (no publisher), 1926.

Reincke-Bloch, Hermann, *Fichte und der deutsche Geist von 1914.* Rostock, H. Markentien, 1915.

Rickert, Heinrich, "Die philosophischen Grundlagen von Fichtes Sozialismus," *Logos.* Vol. 11 (1922/23), pp. 149-180.

Rickert, Heinrich, "Fichtes Atheismusstreit," *Kantstudien,* vol. iv, 1900.

Ritzer, Franz, *Fichtes Idee einer Nationalerziehung und Platons paedagogisches Ideal.* Langensalza, Beyer, 1913.

Rose, J. H., *Nationality in Modern History,* Lect. 3 and 7. New York, Macmillan, 1916.

Sachse, Paul, *Fichtes nationalökonomische Anschauungen.* Heidelberg, Roessler, 1902.

Santayana, G., *Egotism in German Philosophy.* New York, 1916.

Scherr, Johannes, *Menschliche Tragikomödie.* Vol. viii, "Fichte." 3d edition, Leipzig, Wigand, 1884.

Schmidt, Erich, *Fichtes Reden an die deutsche Nation.* Berlin, Gustav Schade, 1908.

Schmoller, Gustav, "Johann Gottlieb Fichte. Eine Studie aus dem Gebiete der Ethik und der Nationalökonomie," in *Jahrbücher fuer Nationalökonomie und Statistik.* Vol. v (1865), pp. 1-61.

Schneider, Fritz, *Fichte als Sozialpolitiker.* Halle, C. A. Kämmerer, 1894.

Scholz, Heinrich, "Fichte und Napoleon," *Preussische Jahrbücher.* Vol. 152 (1913), pp. 1-12.

Schwarz, Heinrich, *J. G. Fichtes, des deutschen Kraftmannes, Lebensweisheit und vaterländische Gedanken.* Berlin, Nicolai, 1860.

Schwarz, Hermann, "Einführung in Fichtes Reden an die deutsche Nation," *Pädagogisches Magazin.* No. 967, Langensalza, 1924.

Schwenger, Rudolf, *Der Begriff der bürgerlichen Gesellschaft bei Kant und Fichte.* Bonn, Sceur, 1929.

Siemsen, A., "Der missbrauchte Fichte," *Zeitschrift für Völkerfriede.* vol. 19, January, 1919, pp. 3-4.

Smith, William, *Memoir of Gottlieb Fichte.* Boston, James Munroe, 1846.

Soanen, H., "La Franc-Maçonnerie et l'armee pendant la Révolution et l'Empire," *Annales Historiques de la Révolution Française.* Vol. 5 (1928), pp. 530-540.

Spranger, Eduard, "Altensteins Denkschrift von 1807 und ihre Beziehungen zur Philosophie," *Forschungen zur Brandenburgisch und Preussischen Geschichte.* Vol. 18 (1905), 471-517.

Staehler, Paul, *J. G. Fichte, ein deutscher Denker.* Berlin, L. Simon Nf., 1914.

Stock, Otto, "Johann Gottlieb Fichte als Herold und Vorbild echter Vaterlandsliebe," *Neue Jahrbücher fuer das Klassische Altertum.* vol. viii (1901), pp. 1-10.

Storrs, Margaret, *The relation of Carlyle to Kant and Fichte.* Bryn Mawr, Pa., 1929.

Trautwein, Carl, *Über Ferdinand Lassalle und sein Verhältnis zur Fichteschen Sozialphilosophie.* Jena, G. Fischer, 1913.

Treitschke, Heinrich von, *Fichte und die nationale Idee (1862),* Historisch und Politische Aufsätze, I—Leipzig, S. Hirzel, 1886 (5th edition), pp. 113-142.

Trendelenburg, Adolf, *Zur Erinnerung an Johann Gottlieb Fichte.* Berlin, Akademie der Wissenschaften, 1862.

Ueberweg, Friedrich, *Grundriss der Geschichte der Philosophie.* 12th edition, Berlin, E. S. Mittler, 1923, vol. iv, pp. 11-35.

Vogel, Paul, *Fichtes philosophisch-paedagogische Ansichten in ihrem Verhältnis zu Pestalozzi.* Langensalza, 1907.

Vorkämpfer der deutschen Freiheit. No. 24, Munich, Nationalverein, 1911.

Wallner, Nico, *Fichte als politischer Denker.* Halle, Niemeyer, 1926.

Walz, Gustav Adolf, *Die Staatslehre des Rationalismus und der Romantik und die Staatsphilosophie Fichtes.* Berlin-Grunewald, Walther Rothschild, 1928.

Weber, Marianne, *Fichtes Sozialismus und sein Verhaeltnis zur Marxschen Doktrin.* Volkswirtschaftliche Abhandlungen der Badischen Hochschule, vol. 4, no. 3, 1900 (also in book form).

This study by the wife of Max Weber has an amusing foreword in which the eminent professor assures the readers that it is really and in fact the work of his wife and not written by him for his wife.

Windelband, Wilhelm, *Fichtes Idee des deutschen Staates.* Rede zur Feier des Kaisers Geburtstages, 27. Januar 1890. Freiburg, J. C. B. Mohr, 1890.

Wundt, Max, *Fichte Forschungen.* Stuttgart, Fr. Frommanns Verlag, 1929.

Zeller, E., " Johann Gottlieb Fichte als Politiker," in *Historische Zeitschrift.* Vol. ix (1860), pp. 1-35.

OTHER SECONDARY WORKS

Bagger, Eugene, *Francis Joseph.* New York, Putnam, 1927.

Barruel, Augustin de, *Mémoires pour servir à l'histoire du Jacobinisme.* Hambourg, P. Fauché, 1803.

Bernhardi, Friedrich von, *Germany and the Next War.* New York, Longmans, Green, 1914.

Bismarck, Otto von, *Die politischen Reden des Fürsten Bismarcks.* Vol. i, Stuttgart, Cotta, 1892.

Brinton, Crane, *The Jacobins.* New York, Macmillan, 1930.

Burke, Edmund, *A Philosophical Inquiry into the Origin of our Ideas of the Sublime and Beautiful.* London, G. Bell & Sons, Ltd., 1913.

Couzinet, *Le Prince de Machiavelli et la théorie de l'absolutisme.* Ch. 5, Paris, 1910.

Croce, Benedetto, *A History of Italy, 1871-1915* (English translation). Oxford, Clarendon Press, 1929.

Fisher, H. A. L., *The republican tradition in Europe.* New York and London, Putnam, 1911.

Gettell, Raymond G., *History of Political Thought.* New York, Century, 1924.

Gooch, G. P., *Germany and the French Revolution.* London, Longmans, Green, 1920.

Grandvilliers, Jean de, *Essai sur le libéralisme allemand.* Paris, Biard et Brière, 1914.

Guilland, Antoine, *Modern Germany and her historians.* London, Jarrold, 1915.

Haupt, Hermann, " Die Jenaische Burschenschaft von der Zeit ihrer Gruendung bis zum Wartburgfeste." *Quellen und Darstellungen zur Geschichte der Burschenschaften und der deutschen Einheitsbewegung.* Vol. i, pp. 18-113, Heidelberg, Carl Winter, 1910.

Hauptmann, Gerhart, *Festspiel in deutschen Reimen, Zur Erinnerung an den Geist der Freiheitskriege der Jahre 1813, 1814, 1815. Aufgeführt bei der Jahrhundertfeier in Breslau, 1913.* Berlin, S. Fischer, 22d edition, 1913.

Haeusser, Ludwig, *Deutsche Geschichte.* Vol. 3, Berlin, Weidmann, 1856.

Hayes, Carlton J. H., *Essays on Nationalism.* New York, Macmillan, 1926.

Hayes, Carlton, J. H., *The Historical Evolution of Modern Nationalism.* New York, Richard R. Smith, 1931.

Haym, Rudolf, *Die romantische Schule. Ein Beitrag zur Geschichte des deutschen Geistes.* 3d edition, 1914, Berlin, Weidmannsche Buchhandlung.

Henderson, Ernest F., *A Short History of Germany.* 2 vols., New York, Macmillan, 1902.

Houben, H. H., *Verbotene Literatur von der klassischen Zeit bis zur Gegenwart.* 3 vols., Bremen, Schuenemann, 1928, vol. 2, pp. 83-248: " Fichte."

Howard, Milford W., *Fascism a challenge to democracy.* New York and Chicago, Revell, 1928.

Ilse, L. Fr., *Geschichte der politischen Untersuchungen, welche durch die neben der Bundesversammlung errichteten Commissionen, der Central—Untersuchungs—Commission zu Mainz und der Bundes—Central—Behörde zu Frankfurt in den Jahren 1819 bis 1827 und 1833 bis 1842 geführt sind.* Frankfurt a/M.—Meidinger Sohn, 1860.

Kirkup, Thomas, *History of Socialism.* 5th edition, London, A. C. Black, 1920.

Lamprecht, Karl, *Deutsche Geschichte.* Vol. iii, p. 3, Berlin, Weidmann, 1907.

Lenz, Max, " Nationalempfinden im Zeitalter unserer Klassiker, Vortrag, 1915." *Jahrbuch der Goethe Gesellschaft.* N. S. vol. 2 (1915), Leipzig, Insel Verlag.

McGiffert, A. C., *The Rise of Modern Religious Ideas.* New York, Macmillan, 1915.

Madelin, Louis, *The French Revolution* (English trans.). New York, Putnam, 1923.

Marx, Karl, *Revolution und Kontre-Revolution* (translated from the English). Stuttgart, Dietz, 1919.

Meinecke, Friedrich, *Das Zeitalter der deutschen Erhebung, 1795–1815.* Bielefeld, Velhagen, 1906.

Meinecke, Friedrich, *Weltbürgertum und Nationalstaat. Studien zur Genesis des deutschen Nationalstaates.* Munich and Berlin, R. Oldenbourg, 5th edition, 1919.

Oncken, Hermann, "Deutsche geistige Einflüsse in der europäischen Nationalitätenbewegung des 19. Jahrhunderts," *Deutsche Vierteljahrsschrift für Literaturwissenschaft und Geistesgeschichte.* Vol. 7, 1929, pp. 607-627.

Ranke, Leopold von, *Zur eigenen Lebensgeschichte. Sämtliche Werke.* Vols. 53-54, Leipzig, Duncker und Humblot, 1890.

Rapp, Adolf, *Der deutsche Gedanke. Seine Entwicklung im politischen und geistigen Leben seit dem 18. Jahrhundert.* Bonn und Leipzig, Kurt Schroeder, 1920.

Robison, John, *Proofs of a Conspiracy.* New York, G. Forman, 1798.

Rogers, A. K., *A Student's History of Philosophy.* New York, Macmillan, 1918.

Rose, J. H., *Cambridge Modern History.* Vol. 9, pp. 325-328.

Ruggiero, Guido de, *The History of European Liberalism.* London, Oxford Press, 1927.

Scherr, Johannes, *Deutsche Kultur- und Sittengeschichte.* 8th edition, Leipzig, Wigand, 1882.

Schevill, Ferdinand, *The Making of Modern Germany.* Chicago, A. C. McClurg, 1916.

Schlegel, August Wilhelm, *Vorlesungen über schöne Literatur und Kunst, 1801–1804.* In *Deutsche Literaturdenkmale des 18. und 19. Jahrhunderts.* Vol. 17, Heilbronn, Henninger, 1884.

Schurz, Carl, *The Reminiscences of Carl Schurz.* 3 vols., New York, McClure, 1907.

Seeley, John Robert, *Life and Times of Stein.* 3 vols., Cambridge University Press, 1878.

Simkhovitch, Vladimir G., "Approaches to History," II, *Political Science Quarterly.* Vol. 45, Dec. 1930, pp. 481-526.

Taylor, G. R. Stirling, *Modern English Statesmen.* New York, McBride, 1921.

Treitschke, Heinrich von, *Deutsche Geschichte im 19. Jahrhundert.* Leipzig, S. Hirzel, 1879.

Tschuppik, Karl, "Heinrich von Treitschke und die Folgen," *Neue Rundschau.* Vol. 42 (1930), pp. 145-159.

Varnhagen von Ense, Karl August, *Denkwürdigkeiten und Vermischte Schriften.* 2d ed., 9 vols. in 5, Leipzig, Brockhaus, 1843-1859.

Wechssler, Eduard, "Die Auseinandersetzung des deutschen Geistes mit der französischen Aufklärung (1732-1832)." *Deutsche Viertel-*

jahrschrift für Literaturwissenschaft und Geistesgeschichte. Vol. i (1923), pp. 613-635.

Wenck, Waldemar, *Deutschland vor hundert Jahren. Politische Meinungen und Stimmungen bei Anbruch der Revolutionszeit.* Leipzig, Grunow, 1887.

Wertheimer, Mildred, *The Pan-German League.* New York, 1924.

INDEX

A

Altenstein, Freiherr von, and the *Reden*, 129

Althusius, Johannes, 40n

Archenholtz, J. W. von, and French Revolution, 54

Army: Fichte's criticism, 100-101; and the state, 61

Arndt, Ernst Moritz, and the *Reden*, 130

Arnold, Matthew, and Fichte, 28

Asia, and Europe, Fichte's conception, 89-90

Atheism, charge against Fichte, 21-23, 70-72

Aufruf an mein Volk, Fichte's reaction, 138-142

B

Babeuf, François, 82

Barruel, Abbé, and Jacobinism, 195-196, 200

Bassenitz, and the *Reden*, 132

Benecke, G. F., 127

Bentham, Jeremy, 32

Berlin: Fichte's stay, 24; Masonic lodge, 198

Berlin university: Fichte's plans for, 107; Fichte's resignation and the *Reden*, 126

Bernhardi, Friedrich von, and Fichte, 159, 175

Beyme, K. F. von, and Fichte, 124

Bismarck, Otto von, and German national historiography, 176n

Brandes, J. C., and the French Revolution, 54

Bucholz, P. F., 127

Burschenschaften and Fichte, 160-161, 163, 177

Burke, Edmund, and the French Revolution, 49n, 55-56

C

Calvin, John, 40n

Carlyle, Thomas, and Fichte, 28, 43

Censorship: and Machiavelli, 109; Prussian, 44-45; and the *Reden*, 131, 162

Church: and nationalism, 103-106; and political rights, 49-50; and state, 34, 61-62, 140

Climate, and nationalism, 114

Cosmopolitanism: and Fichte, 150-154, 157-158; in Germany, 147-149; and patriotism, 74-75, 91, 95-100

Culture, and nationalism, 119, 152-153

D

Danton, Georges, 82, 193

Davoust, Marshall, and Fichte, 126

Delbrück, J. F., and the *Reden*, 130

Democracy, and Fichte, 19-20, 25, 30, 70-71

Deutscher Fichte Bund, 185-186

Dewey, John, interpretation of Fichte, 10

Dresch, G. L., and the *Reden*, 132

E

Ebert, Friedrich, and Fichte, 186

Economic liberalism, Fichte's ridicule of, 143

Economics, and the state, 35, 76-82

Education: Fichte's emphasis on, 32, 35, 73-74; and nationalism, 92-93, 99, 113-114, 118, 146; physical, Fichte's plans, 119; and and state, 35, 92, 107

Elections, in Fichte's state, 37

Encyclopaedia (French), work of Freemasonry, 192

Encyclopaedists, and Machiavelli, 108

Enlightenment, influence on Fichte, 16

Ephors, in Fichte's state, 39-40, 68, 137-138

Erlangen university: Fichte's idea of organization, 91-93; Fichte as teacher, 24

215